PENGU

TEACH YOUR

Edward de Bono invented the concept of lateral thinking. A world-renowned writer and philosopher, he is the leading authority in the field of creative thinking and the direct teaching of thinking as a skill. In the decades since Dr de Bono introduced lateral thinking, the concept has become so entrenched in our language that it is used equally in physics lectures, television comedies or brainstorming sessions. His key contribution has been his understanding of the brain as self-organising system. His work spans generations, continents and belief systems, and is equally influential in the boardrooms of leading businesses such as Apple and British Airways as on the shelves of classrooms in rural Africa.

Dr de Bono has written more than sixty books, in forty languages, with people now teaching his methods worldwide. He has chaired a special summit of Nobel Prize laureates, had faculty appointments at the universities of Oxford, London, Cambridge and Harvard, and been hailed as one of the 250 people who have contributed most to mankind.

Dr de Bono's classic bestsellers include *Six Thinking Hats*, *Lateral Thinking, I Am Right You Are Wrong*, *How To Be More Interesting*, *Teach Yourself To Think*, *Teach Your Child How To Think,* and *Simplicity*.

www.edwdebono.com

Other De Bono titles published by Penguin

How To Be More Interesting

I Am Right You Are Wrong

Lateral Thinking

Simplicity

Six Thinking Hats

Teach Your Child How to Think

Edward de Bono

Teach Yourself to Think

PENGUIN BOOKS

PENGUIN BOOKS

Published by the Penguin Group
Penguin Books Ltd, 80 Strand, London WC2R ORL, England
Penguin Group (USA) Inc., 375 Hudson Street, New York, New York 10014, USA
Penguin Group (Canada), 90 Eglinton Avenue East, Suite 700, Toronto, Ontario, Canada M4P 2Y3
(a division of Pearson Penguin Canada Inc.)
Penguin Ireland, 25 St Stephen's Green, Dublin 2, Ireland (a division of Penguin Books Ltd)
Penguin Group (Australia), 250 Camberwell Road, Camberwell, Victoria 3124, Australia
(a division of Pearson Australia Group Pty Ltd)
Penguin Books India Pvt Ltd, 11 Community Centre, Panchsheel Park, New Delhi – 110 017, India
Penguin Group (NZ), 67 Apollo Drive, Rosedale, North Shore 0632, New Zealand
(a division of Pearson New Zealand Ltd)
Penguin Books (South Africa) (Pty) Ltd, 24 Sturdee Avenue, Rosebank, Johannesburg 2196, South Africa

Penguin Books Ltd, Registered Offices: 80 Strand, London WC2R ORL, England

www.penguin.com

First published by Viking 1995
Published in Penguin Books 1996
This edition produced for The Book People Ltd,
Hall Wood Avenue, Haydock, St Helens, WA11 9UL
1

Printed in England by Clays Ltd, St Ives plc

ISBN: 978–0–241–95360–0

www.greenpenguin.co.uk

Contents

Why?

I breathe. I walk. I talk. I think.

I do not have to think about these things, so why should I think about thinking? Thinking is natural. You pick it up as you go along. Intelligent people can think without having to learn to think. Other people cannot think no matter what they do. What is wrong with that view?

Because . . .

Because thinking is the most fundamental human skill.

Because your skill in thinking will determine your happiness and your success in life.

Because you need thinking to make plans, take initiatives, solve problems, open up opportunities and design your way forward.

Because without the ability to think you are like a cork floating along on a stream with no control over its destiny.

Because thinking is fun and enjoyable – if you learn how to make it so.

Because thinking and intelligence are quite separate. Intelligence is like the horsepower of a car. Thinking is like the skill of the car driver. Many highly intelligent people are poor thinkers and get caught in the 'intelligence trap'. Many less intelligent people have developed a high degree of skill in thinking.

Because thinking is a skill that can be learned, practised and developed. But you have to want to develop that skill. You need to learn how to ride a bicycle or drive a car.

Because traditional education at school and university only teach one aspect of thinking.

What about feelings and values?

You may believe that feelings and values are the most important things in life.

You are right.

That is why thinking is so very important.

The purpose of thinking is to deliver to you the values you seek just as the purpose of a bicycle is to get you to where you want to go. A bicycle uses less energy, gets you there faster and allows you to go much further. So thinking allows you to enjoy your values more effectively.

You are locked in a room. You desperately want to get out. You want freedom. Your feelings are very strong. Which is the more useful, this very strong feeling or a key to the lock?

Feelings without the means to carry them out are not much good. At the same time, the key without the desire to leave the room is also not much good.

We need values, feelings and thinking. Feeling is no substitute for thinking. Thinking without values is aimless.

This book is about thinking. Values and feelings are equally important but insufficient without thinking.

Foreword

In writing this book I had to choose between writing a complicated and comprehensive book which would cover all aspects of thinking and writing a much simpler and more accessible book. In the end, the decision was made by the title of the book: *Teach Yourself to Think*. This was to be a book for anyone who was interested in further developing his or her skill in thinking. Few people would be interested in picking up or reading through a complicated book. So I have chosen to keep it simple and practical.

I know from experience that some commentators are terribly upset by simplicity. Such people feel that something simple cannot be serious. Such people are also frightened of simplicity because it threatens the complexity which it is their job to explain. If something is indeed simple then they are without a job.

My preference has always been for simplicity. I have always sought to make things as simple as possible. That is why the thinking 'tools' that I designed have been taught equally to six-year-olds in rural black schools in South Africa and to the top executives of the world's largest corporations.

The very widely used *Six Thinking Hats* framework is very simple in principle but very powerful in use. The framework provides a practical alternative to the traditional argument system that has been in use for 2,500 years. That is why this framework is now being taken up both in education and in business and government areas.

The *L-Game* was invented as a result of a challenge by a famous Cambridge mathematician, Professor Littlewood, to invent a game in which each player had only one playing piece. The game has now been analysed on computer and is a 'real game' (no winning strategy which the first player could use). I recently invented an even simpler game, *The Three-spot Game*.

Above all, simplicity is easy to learn and to use.

Who will be the readers of this book? Over the years I have written many books on thinking and it is impossible to predict who the readers will be. The letters I have received suggest that the readers range very widely indeed. The common thread is motivation and an interest in thinking. I believe that the mass media (TV, radio and press) seriously underestimate the intelligence of the mass market and believe that this market only wants fun and moment-to-moment distraction. That has not been my experience.

There are people who are very complacent about their thinking. Such people believe they have nothing to learn. They usually win arguments and believe there is nothing further to thinking than having and defending a point of view.

There are people who are highly intelligent and do not make mistakes in their thinking. They believe that intelligence is enough and that thinking without mistakes is good thinking.

There are people who have given up on thinking. They have not done particularly well at school and they are no good at solving 'puzzles'. So they come to believe that thinking is not for them. They are content to get by, day to day, as best they can.

Complacency is the enemy of all progress. So is resignation. If you believe you are perfect, then you make no effort to get better. If you have given up, you also make no effort.

This book is directed at those who feel that thinking is an everyday, practical, messy and confusing matter. They want to improve their thinking in order to make it simpler and more effective. They want to have thinking as a skill which they can direct to any matter they choose.

Introduction

I advise you to skip this section. It is rather more complicated than the rest of the book and may give you the wrong impression about the rest of the book. For some readers, however, I need to include this section to point out why our traditional thinking habits are excellent but inadequate. The rear wheels of a motor car are excellent but inadequate on their own. We have developed one aspect of thinking and we are very proud of this and very happy with this. It is time we realized that this aspect is excellent but inadequate.

This introduction is also necessary to 'frame' the rest of the book.

Imagine a kitchen in which a lot of food is piled up on a table in the centre of the room. The cook proceeds to cook or 'process' the food. The cook is very skilful and makes a good job of it. There are no mistakes in the cooking.

Then we ask: how was this food chosen; how was it grown; how was it packaged; how was it brought to the kitchen? In other words we shift attention from the cooking process to the ingredients themselves.

It has been the same with thinking. We have paid a lot of attention to the 'processing' part of thinking. We have developed excellent mathematics, statistics, computers and all the various forms of logic. You feed in the ingredients, the processing takes place and out comes the result. But we have paid far less attention to where the ingredients come from. How were they chosen and how were they packaged?

The ingredients for thinking are provided by *perception*. Perception is the way we look at the world. Perception is the way we carve up the world into chunks that we can handle. Perception is the choice of matters to consider at any one time. Perception chooses whether to regard a glass as half empty or half full.

Most of everyday thinking takes place in the perception stage of thinking. It is only in technical matters that we apply such processes as mathematics.

In the future, computers will probably take over all the processing aspects of thinking, leaving to humans the extremely important aspect of perception. The excellence of processing in the computers will not make up for inadequacies in perception. So the perception part of thinking will be even more important in the future.

Most of the errors of thinking, outside puzzles, are not errors of logic at all but errors of perception. We see only part of a situation. Or, we see a situation only in one particular way. Yet we have persisted in believing that logic is the most important part of thinking and have done almost nothing about perception. There are reasons for this.

When Western thinking habits were being established at the end of the Dark Ages and the beginning of the Renaissance, much of the thinking was being done by church people, since they were the only group that had maintained throughout the

Dark Ages an interest in scholarship and thinking. Also, at that time, the church was very dominant in society and ran universities, schools, etc. So the 'new thinking' that came in with the Renaissance was mainly applied to theological matters and to dealing with heresies. In such areas there were tight definitions of 'God', 'justice' and such matters. It became a matter of working 'logically' with such fixed definitions. So perception was not an important part of this sort of thinking. Perception was also far too subjective in such theological matters. There had to be basic agreement on the starting terms.

We have also believed that *logic* itself should be able to sort out perceptions. This is rubbish because logic is an enclosing system which can only work with what is there. Perception is a generative system which opens up to what is not there. This misconception about the power of logic is one of the major faults of traditional thinking. The misconception arises from the failure to distinguish between foresight and hindsight. It is perfectly true that in hindsight logic can point out inadequacies in perception but that is not the same as pointing out these inadequacies in the first place.

Every valued creative idea will always be totally logical in hindsight. The numbers 1 to 100 can be added together in about five seconds using an idea that is completely logical in hindsight – but getting to that idea needs creativity.

What are the chances of an ant on the trunk of a tree getting to one particular leaf? At every branch point the chances diminish because the ant might have taken one of the other branches. In an average tree the chances are about 1 in

8,000. Now imagine the ant sitting on that leaf. What are the chances of that ant getting to the trunk of the tree? The chances are 1 in 1 or 100 per cent. If the ant simply goes forwards and never doubles back there are no branches. It is exactly the same with hindsight. What is obvious in hindsight may be invisible in foresight. The failure to realize this is responsible for many of our misconceptions about thinking.

Perhaps the main reason why we have not paid more attention to perception is that until about twenty years ago we had no idea how perception worked. We believed, quite wrongly, that perception and processing both worked in *passive-surface* information systems. In such systems the information and the surface on which the information is recorded are passive and have no activity of their own. There is a need for an external processor to organize the information, to move it around and to extract sense from it.

We now believe that perception occurs in a self-organizing information system operated by the nerve networks in the brain. This means that the information and the surface have their own activity and the information arranges itself as groups, sequences and patterns. The process is similar to rain falling on a landscape and organizing itself into streams, tributaries and rivers. Those interested in such processes should read my books *The Mechanism of Mind** and *I am Right – You are Wrong*.†

*Jonathan Cape, 1969; Penguin Books, 1977.
†Viking, 1992; Penguin Books, 1993.

The Gang of Three

After the fall of Rome in AD 400 there came the Dark Ages in Europe. The learning, thinking and scholarship of the Roman Empire was largely lost. For example, Charlemagne, who at one time was the most powerful ruler in Europe, could not read or write. The Dark Ages ended with the Renaissance, which was triggered by the rediscovery of classic Greek and Roman thinking (partly through Arabic texts coming into Europe through Spain).

This 'new' thinking was a powerful breath of fresh air. Humankind was given a more central position in the universe. Humankind could use logic and reason to work things out instead of having to accept everything as part of a religious faith. Not surprisingly this new thinking was eagerly embraced by the *Humanists* or non-church thinkers. More surprisingly, this new thinking was also embraced by church thinkers. So this new/old thinking became the dominant thinking of Western culture and has remained so to this day.

What was the nature of this new/old thinking? We need to go back to the *Gang of Three* who fashioned this thinking. They lived in Greece in Athens between about 400 BC and 300 BC. This Gang of Three was made up of Socrates, Plato and Aristotle.

SOCRATES

Socrates never set out to be a constructive thinker. His purpose was to attack and to remove 'rubbish'. Most of the arguments in which he was involved (as written up by Plato) ended with no positive outcome at all. Socrates would show that all suggestions offered were false but would not then offer a better idea. Essentially he believed in argument (or dialectic). He seemed to believe that if you attacked what is wrong, then eventually you would be left with the truth. This has left us with our obsession with criticism. We believe that it is much more important to point out what is wrong than to construct what is useful.

PLATO

Plato was an Athenian patrician who, as a young man, knew Socrates. Socrates never wrote anything but Plato wrote up Socrates as a character in dialogues. Plato did not much believe in Athenian democracy, which he believed to be a rabble too easily swayed by populist arguments. Plato seemed to be an admirer of the very fascist Sparta. Plato was influenced by Pythagoras, who had demonstrated ultimate truths in mathematics, and Plato believed there were ultimate truths everywhere if only we looked hard enough for them.

Plato was also reacting against the 'relativism' of some of the Sophists, who believed that something was not good or bad in itself but only in relation to a system. Plato realized that society could never be run on such a complicated basis. Plato was a fascist.

From Plato came our obsession with the 'truth' and the belief that we could establish this logically. This belief has been a powerful motivator to all subsequent thinking.

ARISTOTLE

Aristotle was a pupil of Plato's and also the tutor of Alexander the Great. Aristotle tied everything together as a powerful logical system based on 'boxes'. These were definitions or classifications based on our past experience. So whenever we encountered something we had to 'judge' into which box that thing fitted. If necessary, we analysed the situation down into smaller parts to see if we could fit these into standard boxes. Something was either in a box or 'not' in a box. It had to be one or the other and could not be anything else. From this came a powerful logic system based on 'is' and 'is not' and the avoidance of contradictions.

In summary, from the Gang of Three came a thinking system which was based on:

- analysis
- judgement (and boxes)
- argument
- criticism.

We find our way around by fitting new experiences into the boxes (or principles) derived from the past. This is perfectly adequate in a stable world where the future is the same as the past – but totally inadequate in a changing world where the old boxes do not apply. Instead of judgement we need to design our way forward.

While *analysis* does solve a great many problems, there are other problems where the cause cannot be found and if found cannot be removed. Such problems will not yield to yet more analysis. There is a need for design. We need to design a way forward, leaving the cause in place. Most of the major problems in the world will not be solved by yet more analysis. There is a need for creative design.

The traditional thinking system is very lacking in constructive energy, creative energy and design energy. Description and analysis are not enough.

If this traditional system is indeed so limited, then how is it that Western culture has made such tremendous progress in science and technology?

Plato's search for the truth has been a prime motivating factor. Aristotle's classification has also helped. Socratic questioning and attack has played a part. But by far the most important factor has been the *possibility* system. This is an immensely important part of thinking. The possibility system gives hypotheses in science and visions in technology. That is what has driven Western achievement. Chinese culture, which was far ahead of Western technical culture two thousand years ago, came to a halt because they moved into description and never developed the possibility system.

Even today in schools and universities very little attention is given to the 'possibility' system, which is so very important a part of thinking. This is because there is the belief that thinking is all about the 'truth' and 'possibility' is not truth.

Later in this book I intend to give a lot of attention to the possibility system because it is so very important.

Argument is a rather poor way of exploring a subject because each side soon becomes interested only in winning the argument rather than in exploring the subject. At best there might be a synthesis of thesis (one side) with antithesis (the other side) to give a synthesis, but this is only one possibility amongst many which would otherwise have been designed.

Instead of argument we can have *parallel* thinking* in which all parties seek, in parallel, to explore the subject (for example with the Six Hat framework†).

So we have a traditional thinking system which is excellent as far as it goes but inadequate for the following reasons:

1. It does not adequately deal with 'perception', which is by far the most important part of thinking in everyday affairs.

2. Argument is a poor way of exploring a subject and sets up unnecessary adversarial positions.

3. The 'boxes' derived from the past may not be adequate to deal with a changing world, which is very different from the past.

4. Analysis is insufficient to solve all problems. There is a need to supplement it with *design*.

5. The notion that criticism is enough and that somehow useful progress will be made is absurd.

6. There is insufficient attention to the generative, productive, constructive and creative aspects of thinking.

7. The huge importance of the possibility system is largely ignored.

Nevertheless, I do want to emphasize that the traditional thinking system has value and excellence and its proper place. The danger lies in assuming that it is sufficient and allowing the system to dominate all our intellectual effort. I believe

**Parallel Thinking*, Viking, 1994.
†*Six Thinking Hats*, Penguin Books, 1985.

that our civilization would have been at least 300 or even 400 years further advanced if we had not been trapped by such an unconstructive thinking system. You do not have to agree with me.

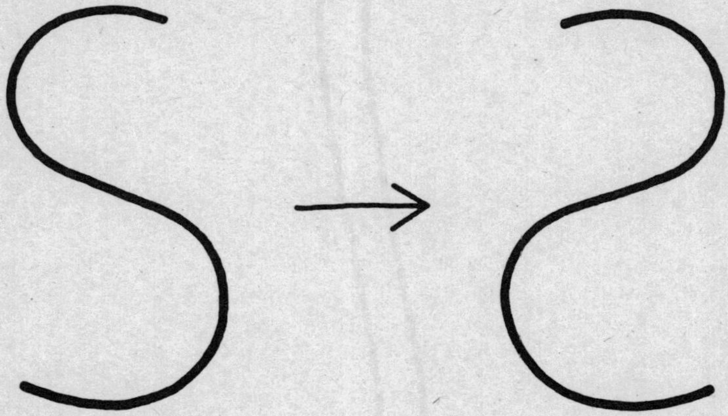

Consider a reversed 'S' shape.

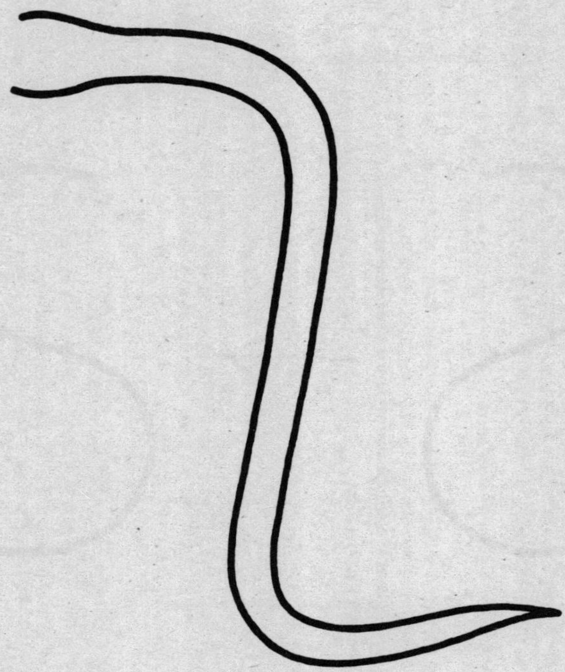

Consider a snake with an open mouth who takes in something at one end and puts out something at the other.

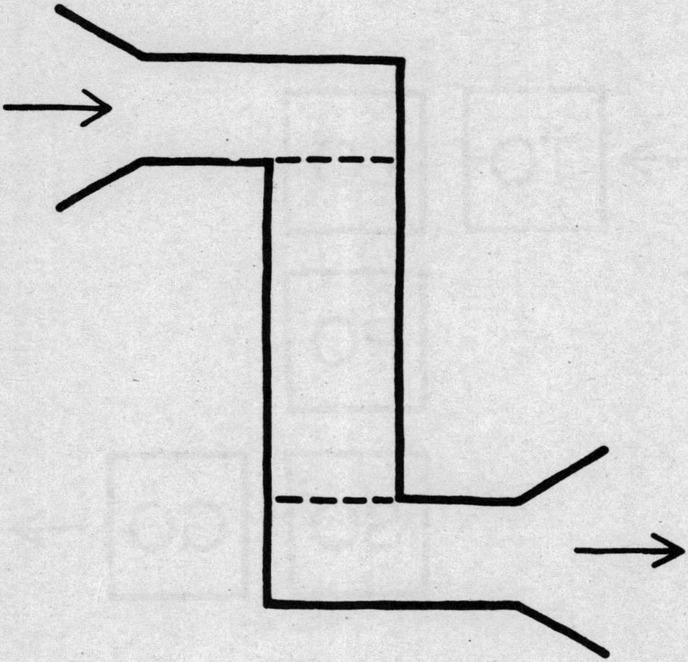

Consider a special type of coffee filter. You put in water at the top and the filtered coffee comes out at the bottom.

Following the perceptions on the previous pages look at the shape shown here. Think of the five boxes as forming a sort of processing pipe. You go in at the top with your intention to think about something. At the bottom out come the results of your thinking. This is the basic diagram which we shall be using for the rest of the book. Keep it clearly in your mind.

You may also regard the two top boxes (**TO** and **LO**) as the 'input' side. The two boxes at the bottom (**SO** and **GO**) are the 'output' side. The bridge or link between input and output is the **PO** box.

The Five Stages of Thinking

This book is based on a five-stage process of thinking. These five stages are not based on an analysis of the normal thinking process. Analysis is useful for description but usually quite useless for operations. It is a mistake to believe that analysis of the thinking process can provide the *tools* necessary for thinking. Tools have to be practical and usable. In the same way, the five stages of thinking used in this book provide a formal framework for the practical operation of thinking. The stages are designed to be practical.

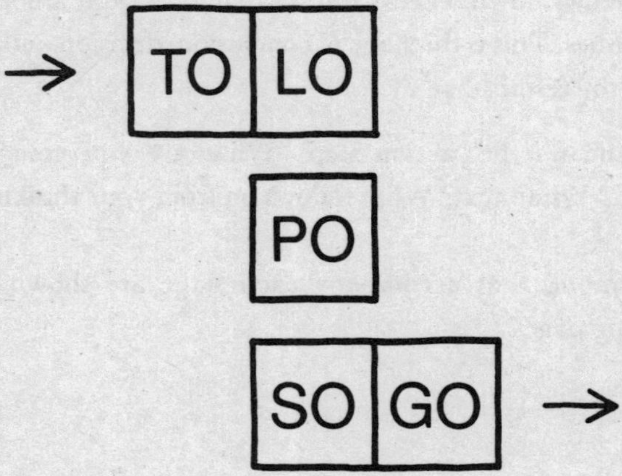

The basic figure that has been considered in the last few pages is shown here again. You enter at the top as shown by the arrow and you exit at the bottom as shown by the arrow. Each of the five boxes contains the word associated with that stage. What do these names mean?

The names of the five stages are outlined below and will be considered much more fully in each section. For each stage there is both a word and also a symbol that indicates in a visual way the nature of that stage.

TO indicates the aim, purpose or objective of the thinking. Where are we going to? With what do we want to end up?

LO indicates the information available and the information we need. What is the situation? What do we know? Perceptions come in here as well.

PO is the stage of possibility. Here we create possible solutions and approaches. How do we do it? What is the solution? This is the generative stage.

SO narrows down, checks out and chooses from amongst the possibilities. This is the stage of conclusion, decision and choice. This is the result stage.

GO indicates the 'action step'. What are you going to do about it? What next? What follows on from your thinking?

The symbols that accompany each stage are shown on the following pages.

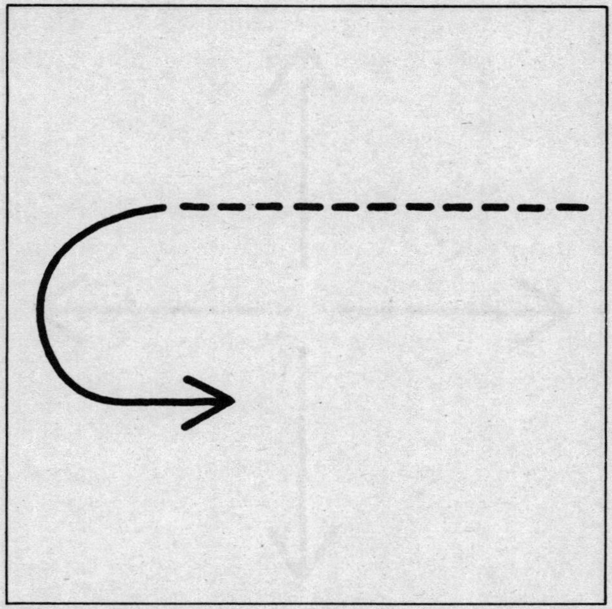

TO symbol

The broken line indicates that we know where we want to go. We pull back from that objective to where we are at the moment. Then with the solid line we seek to move towards the objective. So the symbol indicates a knowledge of the purpose of the thinking and the desire to achieve that purpose.

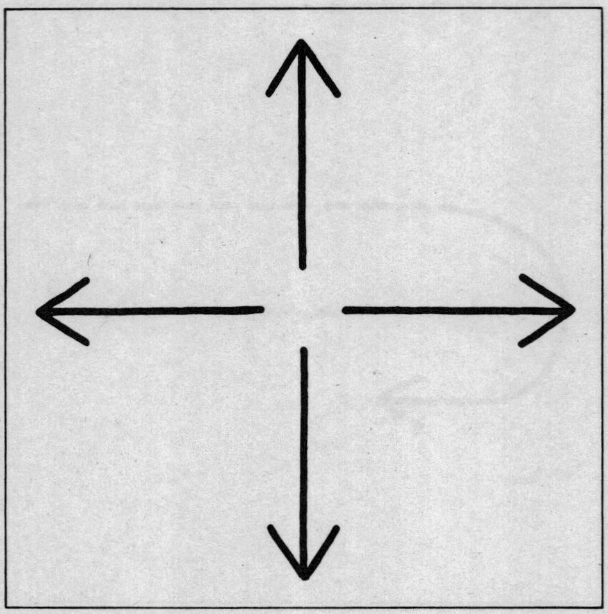

LO symbol

This symbol indicates looking around in all directions. We are looking all around for information. The arrows suggest looking in every direction. What do we see? What information is there?

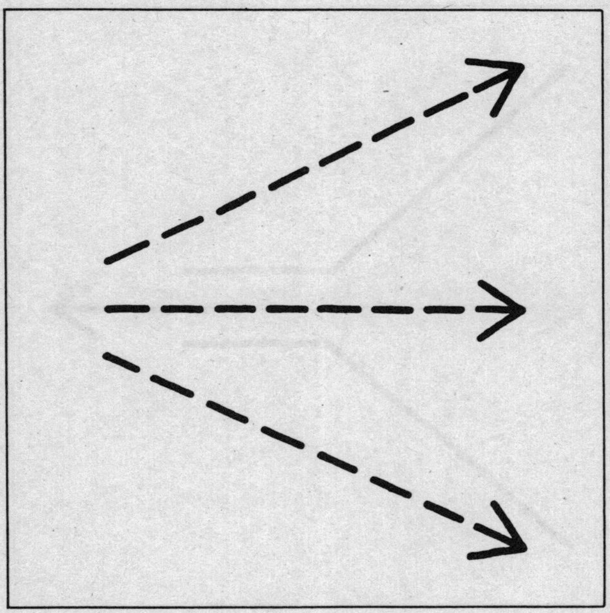

PO symbol

The broken lines indicate *possibility*. This is the stage for creating multiple possibilities. These are not yet lines of action but possibilities that have to be worked out and made solid. There is an emphasis on *more than one* possibility.

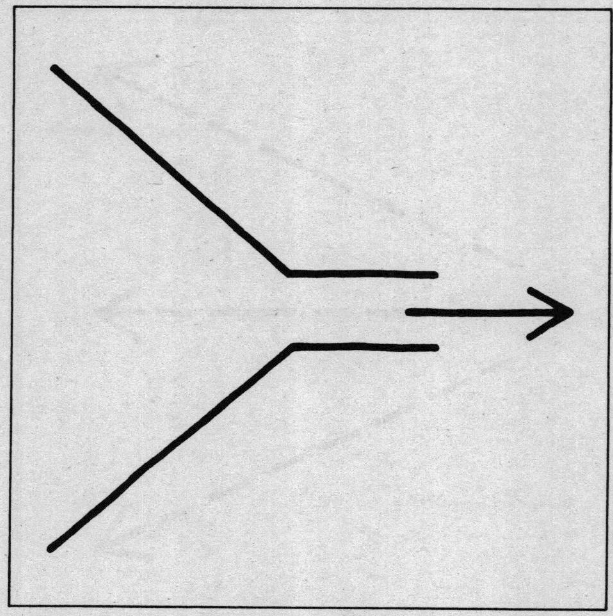

SO symbol

The symbol suggests a narrowing down to one outcome. This illustrates the forming of one usable outcome. Multiple possibilities have now come down to one outcome or result.

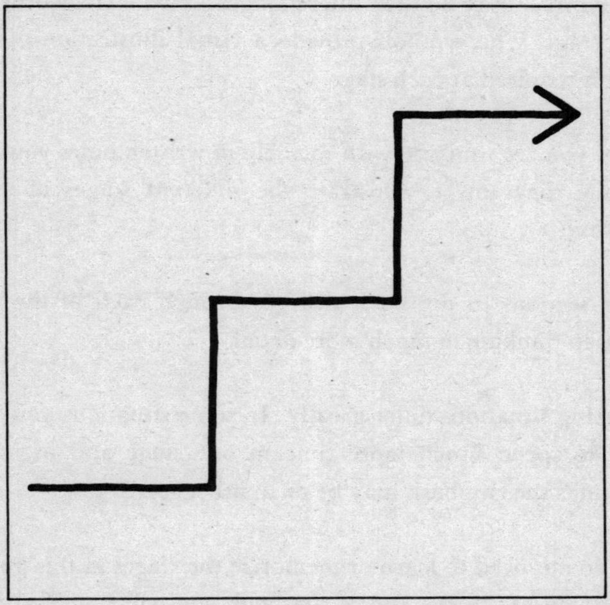

GO symbol

This symbol suggests progressing *forwards and upwards*. This implies positive and constructive action.

The symbols may be used interchangeably with the words for each stage. The symbols provide a visual illustration of the process required at each stage.

When you are thinking with the help of written notes you can use the diagrams to illustrate the different stages of your thinking.

Later sections in the book will go through each of the five stages in thinking in much more detail.

Thinking situations differ greatly. In some situations you will need to spend much more time in one stage and in other situations the emphasis may be on another stage.

You do not need to learn or memorize the stages at this point. When you get to the end of the book you will find that you can remember them very easily: there is an input stage and an output stage and in between is a vertical stack of three thinking stages.

Some Basic Processes in Thinking

It is useful to have an overview of some of the most basic processes in thinking before we look in detail at each of the five stages. These processes come in at every stage so it is useful to have a *preview* of them here.

The basic processes that are going to be considered here are:

1. Broad/specific
2. Projection
3. Attention directing
4. Recognition
5. Movement.

I am aware that these matters can be looked at in many ways. Each of these broad areas could be subdivided and each subdivision could claim to be a basic process in its own right. For the sake of simplicity I have made the above choice.

Broad/Specific, General/Detail

Imagine a short-sighted person seeing a cat for the first time. There is a blurry image and the person sees 'a sort of animal'. As the cat gets nearer the details gradually emerge and now the person gets a true picture of a cat.

Imagine two hawks. One of them has excellent eyesight but the other is short-sighted. Both of them live on a diet of frogs, mice and lizards. From a great height the hawk with excellent eyesight can see and recognize a frog. It dives and eats the frog. Because this hawk has such excellent eyesight it can live on a diet of frogs and soon forgets about mice and lizards.

The hawk with poor eyesight cannot do this. This hawk has to create a *general* concept of 'small things that move'. Whenever it sees a small thing that moves the hawk dives. Sometimes it gets a frog, sometimes a mouse, sometimes a lizard – and occasionally a child's toy.

Most people would immediately regard the hawk with superior eyesight as a superior hawk. In some ways they would be wrong. If frogs died out the first hawk would also die but the second hawk would carry on with very little disturbance. This is because the poor-eyesight hawk has *flexibility*. This flexibility arises from the creation of the general, broad and blurry concept of 'small things that move'.

Some electronic students were given a simple circuit to complete. Ninety-seven per cent of them complained that they did not have enough wire to complete the circuit. Only 3 per cent completed the circuit. The 97 per cent wanted 'wire' and since there was no wire they could not complete the task. The 3 per cent had a broad, general, blurry concept of 'a connector'. Since wire was not available they looked around for another type of connector. They used the screwdriver itself to complete the circuit.

Most of the advantages of the human brain as a thinking

machine arise from its defects as an information machine. Because the brain does not immediately form exact, detailed images we have a stock of broad, general and blurry images which become concepts. These broad, general and blurry images are immensely useful in thinking.

Consider the difference between the following two requests:

- 'I want some glue to stick these two pieces of wood together.'
- 'I want *some way* of sticking these two pieces of wood together.'

The first is very specific. If glue is not available then the task cannot be done. It may also be that glue is not the best way of sticking the pieces together on this occasion.

The second request includes many alternative ways of sticking the two pieces of wood together: glue, nails, screws, clamps, rope, joints, etc. This both allows for flexibility if glue is not available and also allows consideration of the other options.

Good thinkers have this great ability to keep moving from the detail back to the general, from the specific to the broad – and then back again.

When we look for a solution to a problem we often have to consider it in very broad terms first.

'*We need some way of fixing this to the wall.*'

Then we proceed to narrow down the broad to something specific.

In the end we can only 'do' specific things. But the broad, blurry concepts allow us to search more widely, to be more flexible and to evaluate options.

This ability to move from the detail to the general is sometimes called *abstraction* – a term that is more confusing than helpful.

As we go through the five stages of thinking you will see the frequent changes from the broad to the specific and back again.

In thinking we are always urged to be precise. This is one area where you are encouraged to be *broad* and *blurry*. Of course, you have to be 'blurry' in roughly the right direction. If you are looking for 'some way to fix something to the wall' it is not much use looking for 'some way to fry an egg'.

Projection

Imagine that you have a video player in your mind. You press the button and you see played out in your mind a particular scene.

- *Projection* means running something forward in your mind.
- Projection means imagining.
- Projection means visualizing.

We can see things in the world around us. Projection means looking inwards into our minds and seeing things there.

A car is painted white on one side and black on the other side. Imagine what would happen if that car was involved in an accident. In our mind's eye we can see witnesses in court contradicting each other: one declaring the car to be black and another declaring it to be white. Most humour involves projection. We need to imagine the scene.

Projection is a very basic part of thinking because we cannot check out everything in the real world. So we have to 'see what would happen' and to check things out in our minds. We may be wrong and we may not get a very clear picture but at least we can get some indication.

'*What would happen if all public transport were to be free?*'

Someone will imagine the benefits to poorer people. Someone will imagine the overcrowding. Someone will imagine the benefits to in-town shops. Someone may even imagine the cost being put on everyone's taxes.

'*What would happen if a block of ice floating in a glass of water melted? Would the level of water in the glass go up, go down or remain the same?*'

You would need some understanding of physics to answer that question. Our imagination is limited by our knowledge and experience but we have to use it as best we can.

'*What would it look like if we removed that circle and replaced it with a triangle?*'

A designer always has to *project* and visualize what would happen *if* something were to be done.

The famous *thought experiments* used by Einstein depend on

projection. In a thought experiment you run the experiment in your mind and see what happens. You may reach a point when you have to say to yourself that you do not know what would happen. This now becomes a point for further thinking or for carrying out an experiment.

In some cases thinking is indeed carried out with figures and mathematical symbols on paper. We may even play around with words. But most thinking takes place within our minds, using our ability to 'project'.

What you project in your mind is not always right. You may have left out something very important. You may have insufficient knowledge or experience of the subject. You should never be arrogant or dogmatic about your 'projections'. Be willing to accept that they may be wrong or limited.

Attention Directing

'*What time is it?*'

'*How old are you?*'

'*Did you like the soup?*'

'*Do you want some more coffee?*'

'*What is the current exchange rate between the US dollar and the Japanese yen?*'

'*At what temperature does this plastic melt?*'

All questions are attention-directing devices. We could easily drop out 'questions' and instead ask people to direct their attention to specified matters.

'Direct your attention to the time.'

'Tell me the time.'

'Direct your attention to your age and tell me what you find.'

'Direct your attention to the melting-point of this plastic and tell me what you know.'

An explorer returns from an expedition to a newly discovered island. The explorer reports on a smoking volcano and a bird that could not fly. But what else was there? The explorer explains that those were the two things that caught his attention. That was not good enough. So the explorer was sent back with specific instructions to use a very simple attention-directing framework. 'Look north and note what you see. Then look east and note what you see. Then look south and note what you see. Then look west and note what you see. Now come back and give us your notebook.'

The N-S-E-W instructions provided a very simple framework for directing attention. Our attention usually flows in three ways:

1. What catches our interest or emotional involvement at the moment.

2. Habits of attention established through experience and practice.

3. A more or less haphazard drift from one point to another.

A great many of the deliberate processes of thinking involve a specific direction of attention. Socratic questioning is just such a direction of attention. There is nothing magical about it.

The CoRT Thinking Programme for schools (to be described later) includes a number of attention-directing tools. For example the OPV tool asks the thinker to direct his or her attention to the *views of the other people involved*. Some thinkers might have done this automatically. Most do not. So there is a need for a deliberate attention-directing tool.

The important process of *analysis* is an attention-directing instruction.

'*Direct your attention to the component parts making up this situation.*'

'*Direct your attention to the different influences affecting the price of oil.*'

'*Direct your attention to the various factors involved in the effectiveness of a police operation.*'

'*Direct your attention to the parts making up a skateboard.*'

'*Direct your attention to the ingredients of our current strategy.*'

Comparison is another fundamental 'attention-directing instruction'.

'*Direct your attention to the points of similarity between these two proposals.*'

'*Direct your attention to the points of similarity and the points of difference between the two types of packaging.*'

'*Direct your attention to the relative advantages and disadvantages of these two routes to the seaside.*'

'*Compare these two microwave ovens. Direct your attention to how they compare on price, capacity, reputation of maker, service, etc.*'

For attention-directing we can use a deliberate external framework (as with the CoRT tools) or we can use simple internal instructions such as *analyse* and *compare*.

Another form of attention-directing is the *request to focus on some aspect* of a situation.

'*I want you to focus on the political effect of raising the tax on diesel oil.*'

'*I want you to focus on the security arrangements at the banquet.*'

'*I want you to focus on who is going to exercise this dog you want to buy.*'

'*I want you to focus on the benefits of going to a technical college.*'

'*I want you to focus on the disadvantages of taking this fixed-interest mortgage.*'

In the Six Thinking Hats framework (to be discussed later) this focusing is obtained by an external framework. For example, use of the 'yellow hat' implies an exclusive focus on the values and benefits in the situation under discussion. Use of the 'black hat' implies an exclusive focus on the dangers, problems, drawbacks and caution points.

Although most people claim to carry out attention-directing internally, in practice they do not. For example, in a group of highly educated executives one half were asked to judge a suggestion objectively and the other, random, half were asked to use the yellow and black hats deliberately. Those using the hats turned up three times as many points as the others. Yet most of the others would claim always to look at the 'pros and cons' in any situation.

That is why it is sometimes necessary to have external, formal and deliberate attention-directing tools. They may seem simple and obvious but they are effective.

Recognition and Fit

A common child's activity toy consists of a box or board with different-shaped holes in it. The child is required to put different-shaped blocks or pieces into the different-shaped holes. Some fit and some do not fit.

Someone is coming towards you from a distance. You have no reason to expect a particular person. As the person gets closer you begin to think that you might recognize her. She gets close and suddenly you are sure: recognition 'clicks'; there is a 'fit'.

A wine expert tastes wine from a bottle with a masked label. After a while she declares that it is from the Casablanca region in Chile. Recognition and identification have taken place.

The brain forms patterns from experience. Actually experience self-organizes itself into patterns within the brain. That is why we can get dressed in the morning. Otherwise we might have to explore the 39,816,800 ways of getting dressed with just eleven items of clothing. Without patterns we could not cross the road or drive or read or write or do anything useful at work. The brain is a superb pattern-making and pattern-using system (which is why it is so bad at creativity).

We seek to *fit* things into the appropriate pattern. We seek to use the *boxes* and definitions derived from experience – just as Aristotle wanted us to do. We usually call this recognition, identification or judgement. Mostly it is extremely useful. Occasionally it is dangerous, when we trap something in the wrong box or when we seek to use old-fashioned boxes on a changed world.

We set out to look for something. We are very happy when we find something that 'fits' what we are looking for. We look no further.

There is a sort of 'click' about recognition. This really means that we have switched into a well-established pattern and are no longer 'wandering around'.

I prefer the word 'fit' to the word 'judgement' because judgement has a much wider meaning. Judgement may mean evaluation and assessment, which are specific attention-directing processes. The word 'fit' is closer to 'recognition'.

In some ways the purpose of thinking is to abolish thinking. Some people have succeeded in this. The purpose of thinking is to set up routine patterns so that we can always see the world through these routine patterns, which then tell us what to do. Thinking is no longer needed. Some people have succeeded in this because they believe that the patterns they have set up are going to be sufficient for the rest of their lives. There is no prospect of change or progress for such people. But they may be complacent and content.

In thinking we try to move towards 'recognizing' patterns.

We note when we have a recognition. We also need to note the value – or danger – of that recognition. Using stereotypes of people or races is a form of recognition but one that is more harmful than useful.

Movement and Alternatives

The basic thinking processes mentioned up to this point will be familiar to most traditional thinkers but *movement* will not be familiar.

'Movement' simply means 'How do you move forward from this position?'

In its most extreme form movement is used along with provocation as one of the basic techniques of lateral (creative) thinking.

In a provocation we can set up something which is totally outside our experience and even contrary to experience. As a provocation we might say: 'Cars should have square wheels.' Judgement would tell us that this is nonsense: it is structurally unsound; it would use more fuel; it would shake to pieces; speed would be very limited; tremendous power would be needed; the ride would be most uncomfortable, etc., etc. Obviously, judgement would not help us to use that provocation because judgement is concerned with past experience whereas creativity is concerned with future possibility. So we need another mental operation and this is called 'movement'. How do we move forward from the provocation?

We might get movement from imagining the square wheel rolling (the projection process). As the wheel rises on the corner point the suspension could adjust and get shorter so the car remained the same distance from the ground. From this comes the concept of suspension that reacts in anticipation of need. This leads on to the idea of 'active' or 'intelligent suspension', which is now being worked out as a real possibility.

Movement covers all ways of moving forwards from a statement, position or idea. Movement can include *association*. We move from one idea to an association.

Movement can include drift or day-dreaming, in which ideas just follow one another.

Movement also includes the setting up of alternatives. If we have one satsifactory way of doing something why should we seek out alternatives? There is no logical reason therefore we have to make a deliberate effort to generate parallel alternatives. This involves movement: 'How else can we do this?'

The value of seeking further alternatives is obvious. The first way is not necessarily the best way. A range of alternatives allows us to compare and assess them and choose the best.

'Movement' may be directed by an instruction or attention-directing request. We may instruct ourselves to direct attention to 'other members of the same class'. So we move to these other members.

Movement is a very broad process and overlaps with other processes.

Movement is also the basis of 'water logic' which is described in my book *Water Logic*.* In water logic we observe the natural flow from one idea to another. In the more deliberate process of movement we seek to bring about movement from one idea to another.

'*Where do we go to from here?*'

'*What alternatives are there?*'

'*How do we get movement from this provocation?*'

'*What follows?*'

'*What idea comes to mind?*'

It could be said that the whole of thinking is an effort to get 'movement' in a useful direction. We use many devices for that purpose.

* *Water Logic*, Viking, 1993; Penguin Books, 1994.

Frameworks

I intend to outline here two frameworks which I shall be referring to from time to time in the rest of the book. There is no need to know these frameworks. You can simply ignore all references to the frameworks when you come across them. The book will work just as well without them.

There is, however, a need to mention these frameworks in the book because many people familiar with my other work in thinking will wonder how the frameworks they know fit in with this particular book. But making this connection might confuse those readers who did not know anything about the other methods. They would get annoyed and confused when they came across a reference that did not make sense to them. So I am outlining the frameworks here so that readers of this book will be prepared for the references. They can then ignore them if they wish.

It is also possible that readers may then wish to follow up these references and also acquaint themselves with the other material.

At this point you can skip the rest of this section and simply ignore all future references which you do not understand. That will not affect the usefulness of the book.

The Six Thinking Hats

This very simple and powerful framework is now in use in schools and also in business around the world. There are many reasons why the framework has been so widely adopted.

1. It provides an alternative to traditional Western adversarial argument.
2. It is usable across a very wide range of cultures which do not accept Western argument.
3. It is much more creative and constructive than traditional argument.
4. It is very much quicker (an IBM lab reported a reduction in meeting times of 75 per cent).
5. It gets the best out of people.
6. It allows the thinker to do one thing at a time and to do it very thoroughly – instead of trying to juggle all aspects of thinking.
7. It removes the ego and politics from thinking.
8. It provides the 'parallel' thinking needed to design the way forward when traditional 'boxes' are no longer adequate.
9. It is very easy to learn and to use.
10. It is practical.

There are now certified trainers worldwide in the teaching of the Six Hats method. Peter and Linda Low in Singapore have trained over 3,000 people in a very short time. There are also special courses for schools.

There are six imaginary *thinking hats*. Only one is used at a time. When that hat is used then everyone in the group wears the same hat. This means that everyone is now thinking in parallel in the same direction. Everyone is thinking about the subject-matter and not about what the last person said.

The White Hat

Think of white paper and computer printout. The white hat indicates an exclusive focus on information. What information is available? What information is needed? What information is missing? How are we going to get the information we need?

All information is laid down in parallel even if it is in disagreement. The quality of information may range from hard facts which can be checked to rumours or opinions which exist.

The Red Hat

Think of fire and warm. The red hat allows the free expression of feelings, intuition, hunches and emotions without apology and without explanation. The red hat asks a person to express his or her feelings on the subject at this moment in time (later the feelings could change). There must never be any attempt to justify or give the basis for the feelings. Feelings exist and should be allowed into the discussion provided they are signalled as feelings and not disguised as logic. Intuition may be based on a great experience of the field and may be very valuable.

The Black Hat

Think of a judge's robes, which are usually black. The black hat is for *caution* and stops us doing things which are dangerous, damaging or unworkable. The black hat is for risk assessment. The black hat is for critical thinking: why something does not fit our policy, our strategy, our resources, etc.

The black hat is a most useful hat but, unfortunately, is very easy to overuse. Food is good for you but overeating is bad for the health. This is not a fault of the food but of its overuse. In exactly the same way the black hat is very useful and the fault lies only in its overuse. The tendency to overuse the black hat arises directly from the Gang of Three, where Socrates felt it was enough to be negative and the truth would eventually emerge. So there are people who feel that it is enough to be negative.

The Yellow Hat

Think of sunshine and optimism. The yellow hat is the *logical positive* hat. Under the yellow hat the thinker seeks out the values and benefits. The thinker looks to see how the idea can be made workable and put into practice.

The yellow hat is much harder than the black hat and requires much more effort. The brain is naturally tuned to point out what is wrong and what is not as it should be. In order to avoid danger and mistakes we are naturally cautious. The yellow hat requires effort. Often this effort is well rewarded. Suddenly we see values and benefits which we had never noticed before. Without the yellow hat creativity is almost impossible because we would never see the benefits of an emerging idea.

The Green Hat

Think of vegetation, growth, energy, branches, shoots, etc. The green hat is the creative hat. Under the green hat we put forward alternatives. We seek out new ideas. We modify and change suggested ideas. We generate possibilities. We use provocations and movement to produce new ideas.

The green hat is the action hat. The green hat opens up possibilities. The green hat is the productive and generative hat. At the green-hat stage things are only 'possibilities'; they have to be developed and checked out later.

The Blue Hat

Think of blue as sky and overview. The blue hat is the control hat. The blue hat is concerned with the management of the thinking process. The conductor of the orchestra manages the orchestra and gets the best out of the musicians. The ring-master in a circus makes sure that there is no confusion and that things follow in the proper sequence. So the blue hat is for looking at the thinking process itself.

The blue hat is concerned with defining the problem and what is being thought about. The blue hat is also concerned with outcomes, conclusions, summaries and what happens next. The blue hat sets up the sequence of other hats to be used and ensures that the rules of the Six Hat framework are adhered to. The blue hat is the organizer of the thinking process.

USE OF THE HATS

There are two broad methods of using the hats.

A single hat may be used on its own in a meeting or discussion to request a particular type of thinking for a defined time. For example at a certain point further alternatives may be needed. So the facilitator of the meeting asks for 'three minutes of green-hat thinking'. This aligns the thinking of the members of the group so that for three minutes every one of them is seeking to find further alternatives. At the end of the three minutes they return to the discussion. Later there is a need to consider an action proposal so the facilitator requests 'three minutes of black-hat thinking'. For that three minutes everyone focuses on the dangers and potential problems of the action proposal.

In this 'occasional' use the hats become symbols that allow a particular type of parallel thinking to be requested. Everyone now thinks in parallel instead of in the adversarial mode.

In the sequential use, a sequence of hats are used one after the other. The sequence may be pre-set at the beginning or may evolve. With an evolving sequence the first hat is chosen and then when this has been done the next hat is chosen. For inexperienced groups it is much better to use the pre-set sequence to avoid long arguments over which hat is to be used next.

There is no one fixed sequence in which the hats can be used. The sequence will vary with the situation and also with the participants in the thinking. There are some general guidelines which are given in the certified trainer's course. In general, start with a blue hat and end with a blue hat and choose any reasonable sequence in between.

The CoRT Thinking Programme

This programme was designed specifically for the direct teaching of thinking as a school subject. We have had over twenty years of experience with the programme, which is now widely in use around the world in various ways (Canada, USA, Mexico, Venezuela, UK, Ireland, Italy, South Africa, Malaysia, Singapore, Australia and New Zealand). The use may vary from being mandatory across a whole country, as in Venezuela, to use in certain schools or school districts. In Malaysia the MARA senior science schools have been using the programme for ten years.

The essence of the CoRT Thinking Programme is the *tool* approach. This is a very direct approach to the teaching of thinking. Students practise the tools on a variety of short thinking items. They build up skill in the use of the tool, which can then be used on any other situations. Students often take the tools home to help them help their parents make decisions and plans. It is the transfer aspect of the tools that is most important.

The best research on the use of CoRT programme has been done by Professor John Edwards at James Cooke University, Queensland, Australia.

The CoRT programme is designed to be simple and practical. Teachers can quickly learn to teach it and students love it. Whenever CoRT thinking is formally on the curriculum students always choose it as their favourite subject. Perhaps because there is little else in the curriculum that allows free thinking.

The CoRT programme is divided into six sections each of which deals with one aspect of thinking. Each section contains ten lessons.

CoRT 1 – Breadth
CoRT 2 – Organization
CoRT 3 – Interaction
CoRT 4 – Creativity
CoRT 5 – Information and feeling
CoRT 6 – Action

CoRT 1 contains certain basic 'attention-directing' perceptual tools. These are now very widely used. Each tool is assigned a name so that the tool can be learned and used deliberately. These names have a useful perceptual purpose. The names are derived from the initials of the process that is being requested. The basic tools are as follows:

PMI Plus, Minus and Interesting. Direct your attention to the Plus points, then the Minus points and finally the Interesting points. The result is a quick assessment scan.

CAF Consider All Factors. What should we take into account when we are thinking about something? What are the factors involved?

C&S This directs attention to the 'Consequences and Sequels' of the action. The request is for a forward look at what will happen later. Different time-scales can be requested.

AGO What are the Aims, Goals and Objectives? What are we trying to do? What are we trying to achieve? Where are we going?

FIP First Important Priorities. Direct attention to those things which really matter. Not everything is of equal importance. What are the priorities?

APC Alternatives, Possibilities and Choices. Create new alternatives? What are the possibilities? What are the choices?

OPV Direct attention to Other People's Views. Who are the other people involved? What are their views?

The tools are used explicitly and directly. They are a formal way of directing perceptual attention in a defined direction.

'*Do a PMI here.*'

'*Let's start with a CAF.*'

'*What's the AGO?*'

'*Time for an APC.*'

All this may seem artificial but it works. Thinking sometimes has to be made artificial and deliberate otherwise we take it for granted and assume that we do things when in fact we do not do them at all. Most people would claim to look at the consequences of an action but experiments show that a deliberate request to look at consequences with a formal C&S request produces a far better scan. Attention does need directing deliberately. Far too many people assume they are good thinkers when they are not.

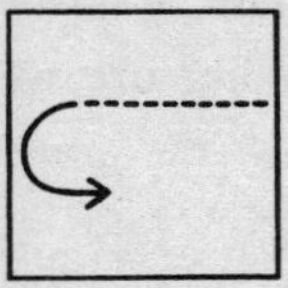

TO

Where Do I Want to Go To?

I am going **to** London
I want **to**
Towards what?
Get **to**
Going **to**
To this destination
To this purpose
To this end
Toward this goal
Get **to** this objective

The word 'to' implies destination and purpose. There is something towards which we are moving. There is somewhere I want to get to.

This first stage of thinking is concerned with purpose.

- 'What is the purpose of my thinking?'
- 'What do I hope to achieve with my thinking?'
- 'What am I thinking about?'

The symbol for the first stage of thinking shows the broken line that comes back from the destination. This indicates that we know the destination. But we have to start towards the destination from where we are at the moment. So the solid line represents our beginning to move to the destination.

The first stage is concerned with the purpose, aim, goal or objective of our thinking. What is the target? What are we aiming for?

In the Six Hats framework the blue hat at the beginning would be used to define the purpose of the thinking and to suggest alternative definitions of the purpose.

In the CoRT Thinking Programme the AGO tool would be used to define the purpose (Aims, Goals, Objectives). A student might be asked to 'do an AGO at this point'. It is interesting that younger students (six to nine years) often have some difficulty with the AGO because it seems to them that all their activity is directed by someone else: 'I do things because I am told to'; 'I do things because I am supposed to.' It is only later that students are comfortable with setting their own goals and purposes. The AGO tool refers to purpose in general and is usually applied to actions or behaviour.

Unfortunately we always assume that the purpose of our thinking is obvious. We know what we are thinking about. In my many years of experience in the field of teaching thinking I have found that a clear definition of purpose is very rare indeed. This is one of the parts of thinking that people do very badly. And yet attention to the clear definition of the purpose of the thinking can make the thinking itself much easier and much more effective. If you do not really know where you want to go you are unlikely to get there. Do not assume that this first stage of thinking is easy or obvious.

Thinking Action

What can you do about the purpose of your thinking?

DEFINE

Spell out the purpose of your thinking even if you believe it to be obvious.

'*Right now the purpose of my thinking is –*'

Spell it out. See if it sounds right. Sometimes just defining the purpose leads you to want to change it.

REDEFINE

When you have spelled out the purpose you may then wish to redefine it.

'*How else can I define this purpose?*'

ALTERNATIVE DEFINITIONS

Attempts to redefine the purpose may quickly lead you to alternative definitions of your purpose. An alternative definition is a parallel definition and the expressed purpose is no longer the same. Redefinition really means another way of expressing exactly the same purpose. In practice the two overlap so much that there is no point in trying to make a distinction.

SMALLER DEFINITION

You can move from a very broad purpose to a much smaller one.

'I want to be happy' can become 'I want to enjoy this weekend.'

This is a process of refocusing. Instead of focusing on the very broad purpose you become much more specific.

LARGER DEFINITION

You can move in the opposite direction, from a specific purpose to a broader purpose.

'I want some glue to stick these two pieces of wood together' might become 'I want some way of sticking these two pieces of wood together.'

There are times when you want to broaden the focus and times when you want to make it specific. In seeking to stick the two pieces of wood together, in the end you would be looking for glue or nails or something specific. You may want to 'travel' in a certain direction but in the end you have to walk, drive or take a bus.

BREAKING IT DOWN

Very often you would want to break down a larger purpose into smaller purposes so that you could handle them more easily.

'I want to think about my holiday', may break down into:

'*I want to see when I can take the holiday.*'

'*I want to see how much I want to spend.*'

'*I want to see what sort of holiday I really want.*'

'*I want to see what is on offer.*'

'*I want to think about planning the holiday.*'

Each of those could become a separate *sub-focus*. We usually have to break purposes down in this way. We may do it without thinking about it. It is much more effective if you do think about it and do it consciously. That way you will not leave things out.

In some cases this breaking down of a large purpose into smaller purposes could be a matter of analysis.

'What are the components of what I am trying to achieve? Can I tackle each one of these on its own?'

CHANGE

At any time during your thinking you can decide to change the 'purpose' of your thinking. You may find that the original definition of the purpose was too broad or too specific. The important point is to make this change consciously – to know that you are doing it.

It is poor thinking just to drift away from the declared purpose to find yourself thinking about something quite different. Creative thinkers often end up thinking about everything except what they have been asked to think about. In arguments, one or other side very often changes the focus in order to make some point he or she wants to make anyway. Arguments rarely stick to the subject but soon drag in all manner of other subjects.

'Up until now this has been the purpose of my thinking . . . but now I am changing the purpose to . . .'

It may become obvious as you start to think about a matter that the original definition of the purpose is too narrow. So change it. But tell yourself, or others, that you are changing it.

THE 'RIGHT' DEFINITION

Many books on problem solving emphasize the importance of finding and using the 'right' definition of the problem. If you find the 'right' definition then solving the problem is easy. This sounds good but is rather dishonest.

The only time you can find the 'right' definition is after you have solved the problem. Then you look back and say: 'If you had defined the problem this way then you would have solved it.'

There is no magic way of finding the 'right' definition – but we can look for it. We can try different definitions until we come to one which we feel is promising. We can even use several different definitions of the problem.

Consider the following situation. A neighbour plays music very loudly at night. This upsets you and you cannot sleep. How might we define the problem? How might we define the purpose of our thinking?

'*How can I stop my neighbour playing this loud music?*'

'*How can I get someone else to stop my neighbour playing this loud music?*'

'*How can I get my neighbour to play music that I like?*'

'*How can I get to like the music my neighbour plays?*'

'*How can I avoid hearing the music even if my neighbour is playing it?*'

'*How can I stop being upset by my neighbour's loud music?*'

'*How can I teach my neighbour a lesson?*'

Each of these is an alternative definition of what might be the purpose of my thinking. They all come back to the same problem. But the different definitions can lead to very different solutions.

- If you want to avoid being upset you might use tranquillizers.
- If you want to avoid hearing the music you might use ear-plugs.
- If you want to teach your neighbour a lesson you might play your own music very loudly.
- If you want to get someone else to stop the neighbour you might join forces with other neighbours or call the police.
- If you want your neighbour to play music you like then you might try giving your neighbour CDs of your kind of music.

You might observe that each of these definitions of the problem is also a 'way' of approaching that problem. We could classify these approaches as follows:

1. Stop the music
2. Change the music
3. Not hear the music
4. Not mind the music.

All these are problems in their own right (how do we do it?)

but they are also approaches to the overall problem.

This is part of what I sometimes call 'The Concept Fan'.

The Concept Fan

At the right-hand side of the paper we put down the overall purpose of our thinking. Then we see what broad concepts, directions or approaches might get us to that purpose. Then we take each of these as a destination in its own right and see what alternative concepts or routes might get us there. Finally we seek alternative ways of carrying out the concepts.

So the overall problem might be 'traffic congestion in cities'. The different approaches might be:

1. Reduce traffic
2. Get better flow on existing roads
3. Provide more travel space.

Each one of these now becomes a 'thinking purpose' in its own right. How do we reduce traffic?

We might reduce traffic in a number of ways:

1. Discouraging motorists
2. Banning certain types of traffic
3. Providing alternatives that carry more people for the same road space (buses, etc.)
4. Rewarding motorists for keeping out of the city.

We then seek to tackle each of these as a thinking purpose. How do we discourage motorists?

We might discourage motorists in a number of ways:

1. Charge for driving into the city
2. No parking spaces
3. Heavy fines and towaways for illegal parking
4. Inconvenient one-way streets which make car driving less flexible.

Then we might see how each of these might be carried out.

So the Concept Fan is a way of working backwards by redefining the purpose of the thinking.

Working Forwards

Sometimes we need to work in the opposite direction. We have defined a purpose for ourselves. But this purpose is not the overall purpose. In fact, the purpose we have defined for ourselves is only one of the approaches on the Concept Fan. So if someone was asked to tackle the problem of traffic congestion in cities and immediately started to think about 'reducing traffic', then that person could be asked to define the overall purpose. This would be 'coping with traffic congestion in cities'.

There is a well-established method of doing this by asking 'why'. Why do you want to reduce traffic? The answer would be: 'to cope with the problem of traffic congestion'.

I prefer to say, 'What is the overall purpose? Reducing traffic is only one approach to this purpose.'

Of course you could go on almost for ever. Why do you want to cope with the problem of traffic congestion? To make business more effective. Why do you want to make business more effective? For the economic well-being of the country. Why are you concerned with the economic well-being, etc., etc.?

There is some danger in this process because you can move right out of the problem you are actually tackling into some grand improvement in the world itself.

On one occasion I needed to open a bottle of wine but had no corkscrew. The purpose of my thinking seemed to be: how can I get the cork out of the bottle? I tried various approaches without success. Then I shifted the problem: how can I get the cork out of the neck of the bottle? This lead on to attempts to push the cork down into the bottle. This also failed. At this point I went back to the overall definition of the purpose: how can I get the wine out of the bottle? So, using a screwdriver, I made a central hole in the cork and poured out the wine through the hole.

There is a well-known story told in books on operations research about a building in which people complained about the slowness of the lifts. The engineering solution was going to be very expensive. The cheap solution was to put mirrors around the entrances to the lifts. People now spent so much time looking at themselves and others in the mirrors that no one complained any more.

This story is a good example of 'lateral thinking' but the success of the solution does depend on what the real problem was. If the problem was 'complaints about the slowness of the lifts' then the mirrors did solve the problem by removing the complaints. If the problem was that the slow lifts slowed down work and productivity then the mirror solution would not have helped. In fact, the mirror solution might even have had a negative effect. When workers knew the lifts were slow they might have made fewer trips between floors – when they no longer noticed the slowness of the lifts they might have gone back to making more trips and so reduced productivity.

I often tell the story of the alarm clock in Pasadena, California. I had to get up at 4.30 a.m. to drive into Los Angeles to catch a plane to Toronto. So I set the alarm clock on the table beside my bed in the Pasadena Hilton, to go off at 4.30 a.m. At 4.30 a.m. I was awoken and set about switching off the alarm so that all my neighbours would not also be awoken at an hour which might not have suited them. I tried everything, including disconnecting the electricity supply. Nothing had any effect. The sound continued. I was just about to drown the clock in a basin of water when I suddenly noticed that the sound was coming from my travel clock which I had set and then forgotten all about.

I had defined the problem as: how do I turn off this alarm clock? In hindsight, it is easy to say that I should have defined the problem as: how do I stop this alarm sound?

The Dog-leg Approach

A dog-leg approach is when we do not go directly towards the destination but move off in a very different direction. We get to a new position. From this new position we can very easily move to the destination. This sort of thinking is very difficult indeed because at every moment we judge the value of our thinking according to whether it seems to move us towards the desired destination.

I was once told about a very successful salesman of office copiers. When dealing with a major client for the first time the salesmen would make a deliberate mistake. That seems absurd and totally contrary to what the salesman should have been doing. The mistake would make a bad impression.

In fact, the strategy was very successful. The client was so impressed by the speed and efficiency with which the mistake was put right that the salesman got the order. The client was just as interested in after-sales service and attention, and by making the mistake the salesman was able to demonstrate such things.

There is the famous story of the Irishman who was asked by a tourist for directions to some monument. He replied, 'If I was going there I would not start from here.' This is a perfectly logical reply. It illustrates that where we are right now may not be the best place from which to reach the destination. So we should move to another position – and then, from there, find it easier to get to where we want to go. This is the dog-leg approach.

So now the definition of the purpose of our thinking should be: how do we get into a position from which it will be easier to reach the overall destination? This position then becomes a sort of sub-focus. The difficulty is that defining this sub-focus is not at all easy since it does not lie in the direction of the overall purpose. so we need to be specific about seeking to get to a position from which the next step will be easier.

What I have sought to show in this section is that we can seek the 'right' definition but can never be sure we have found it. The main point is to be flexible and to keep trying redefinitions and alternatives. We can move up and down the Concept Fan. All this is part of the thinking process itself. It is not a matter of being given a problem and 'then' you start thinking about it. There is a great deal of thinking to be done before we even start thinking about how to get to the destination. Time spent in thinking at this stage is very usefully spent. If you head off in the wrong direction a great deal of energy and effort will be wasted.

Constraints and Qualifiers

This is quite a difficult point.

'*I want to think about a holiday.*'

That seems simple enough as a definition of the purpose of the thinking. But is it simple? Or, are there a lot of hidden assumptions and factors that go into the definition?

Is the person going to think about 'any' holiday or only one that fits within his or her price range and time availability? Is the person really going to consider a round-the-world trip on a luxury liner costing $25,000 and taking three months?

Should we assume that these background factors be taken for granted? In the case of the holiday it is not unreasonable to suppose that the holiday should 'fit' the circumstances of the thinker. But the point is much broader than that.

Should the qualifiers and constraints be put in as part of the problem definition?

Does a government say, 'We want ways of increasing revenue' or does it say, 'We want ways of increasing revenue that will not cost us votes'?

Should the person thinking about the holiday really say, 'I want to think about a holiday suitable for my budget and my tastes and my time available'?

The interesting thing is that these qualifiers and constraints could come in at any of the first four stages of thinking.

1. The qualifiers and constraints could come in at the **TO** or purpose stage. Here we use them as part of the definition of the purpose of our thinking.

'*I want to think about a holiday within these budget limits and for this available time.*'

This is very similar to a design brief. A designer of a shop would be told that it must be within a certain budget, create a certain impression, comply with building standards, be bold and original, provide maximum window display yet be elegant, etc., etc. An architect would also be given a brief and would work within that brief. So there is nothing strange about putting qualifiers or constraints in as part of the definition of the thinking purpose.

2. Sometimes factors and considerations come in at the information stage (the **LO** stage). In this stage we are looking around for information. Perhaps it is at this stage that factors such as budget, preferences and available time should be brought in.

It would be at this stage that the shop designer would get estimates on the cost of different materials. It would not be possible for the original design brief to say that the facade 'must be marble and must fit within the $30,000 limit'. The information stage might then show that this is simply not possible. Either the marble goes or the limit goes. The designer would then have to come back to the client and ask for a redefinition of the brief.

The holiday thinker might prefer to feed in budget and time qualifiers at this **LO** or information stage.

3. With creative thinking we do not put in constraints at the beginning. We seek ideas in all directions. When we have some ideas then we seek to bring in the qualifiers and constraints at the **PO** stage to see if the ideas can be 'shaped' by these qualifiers and constraints in order to become usable, practical ideas. So the holiday thinker might be free to think of expensive round-the-world cruises but would then proceed to see whether it would be possible to hop on and hop off the ship for a shorter, less expensive cruise. Or, if the person liked the cruise idea he might look around for a cheaper cruise and might seek ways of getting more holiday time. But if the time and budget had been part of the definition then that person would never have even considered a cruise.

Using the qualifiers and constraints only at this stage means a lot more thinking work. A lot of ideas might be opened up but cannot be shaped into a usable form. But there is the possibility of really new ideas.

4. Finally, the qualifiers and constraints could be brought in during the **SO** stage of thinking. This is the stage that takes the output from the **PO** (possibility stage) and reduces it to a form suitable for action. Judgement, assessment, evaluation take place in the **SO** stage.

So the qualifiers and constraints might be used as part of the evaluation process.

'*This holiday is too expensive. Throw it out.*'

'*This holiday requires more time than is available. Throw it out.*'

Here the thinking is wide-ranging, free and unconstrained, but many of the suggestions reached are then thrown out because they do not fit the constraints.

If you want someone to buy a red pen for you do you specifically ask, 'Please get me a red pen', or do you say, 'Bring me a whole number of different colour pens'? When confronted by the whole range of different colour pens you would then reject all those which were not red. It must seem obvious that the first method of specifying the exact need is much more efficient than the second method of imposing the specifications only at judgement time. There is, however, another aspect. When confronted with the large range you might actually find that you preferred the green pen. You would never have had the option if red had been part of the initial instruction.

Since it is clear that the constraints and qualifiers could come in at any of the first four stages of thinking, what do we do in practice?

There are the following guidelines:

1. If you are interested in new and creative ideas do not put the constraints and qualifiers into the purpose definition.

2. If you are not interested in new ideas, or do not have the time, put a few constraints and qualifiers into the purpose definition but do not overload it.

3. The constraints and qualifiers should always be available in the information (**LO**) stage. You should explore them fully even if you are going to ignore them in the next stage of thinking. There is no justification for leaving them out in this stage.

4. In the assessment (**SO**) stage the constraints and qualifiers must be used in order to end up with a practical usable idea. At the same time you should be willing to 'challenge' these constraints and qualifiers: are they really essential?

Problems

I have a big problem with the word 'problem'.

Far too many people believe that thinking is all about *problem solving*. Thinking is only to be used for problem solving. Why else should we think? Thinking is associated with the unpleasantness and difficulty of problems. That is why so many people do not like the idea of 'thinking'. It is hard. It is difficult. It is to do with problems. If there are no problems, then you do not need to think.

This matter is made far worse by the North American habit of calling all thinking 'problem solving'. This ensues from the following line of thought. There is something that is desired. How to get it is not obvious. Therefore there is a problem to be solved. In my opinion, this very broad use of the word 'problem' is both limiting and dangerous. It usually means that we end up thinking only about problems of the defect type. Cognitive psychologists are also guilty of this use of the word 'problem' and as a result end up studying only problem solving in the belief that they are studying thinking in its much broader sense. Mankind is then called a problem-solving creature, which is a nonsense that leaves out all the creative and constructive and playful instincts that have really contributed to human progress.

In Western organizations 'improvement' usually means getting rid of faults, defects, bottlenecks, high-cost areas, complaint areas and problems. There is something 'wrong' and we have to put it right. This very limiting habit arises from our obsession with 'problems'. If we just get rid of problems then everything will be fine. There is the famous and very dangerous saying: 'If it is not broken, then don't fix it.' This is dangerous because you attend only to problems and when you fix them you are back to where you were before you had the problem. Meanwhile your competitors have been making improvements at points which were not problems and you find that you have been left far behind.

Much of this obsession with problems also comes from the Gang of Three who set Western thinking habits. Socrates set out to show what was wrong. So the 'critical' frame of mind is very dominant. This does have a high usefulness because solving problems certainly leads to improvement. The danger is when we become so obsessed by problem solving that we neglect the creative and generative aspects of thinking.

It has to be said that there are also very practical reasons for our obsession with problems.

1. A problem is like a headache or a stone in your shoe. You know it is there. A problem presents itself. In contrast a creative need never presents itself – you have to bring it into being by defining the need.

2. Very often you are 'forced' to think about problems. It is not a matter of choice. If your car has a puncture you have to do something about it. If the roof is leaking you have to do something about it. If the chip pan in the kitchen catches fire you have to do something about it. Almost all other types of thinking are optional. So they do not get done or only get done after the urgency of problems has been attended to. In business, the urgent comes before the important, so much time is spent on urgent things and very little is left over for the really important things.

3. Perhaps the most important practical reason why we are so obsessed with problems is that solving a problem provides a 'real', visible and predictable benefit. If you remove the stone from your shoe you know the benefit. If you solve the problem of the leaking roof you know the benefit. If you get your printing machine to align the colours correctly you know the benefit. With much of the other types of thinking the benefit is speculative, general or vague. If you have a creative idea you do not know what benefits it will offer, whether it will be practical, whether it will be easy to

implement, whether others will like it, etc. In contrast everyone will accept and be eager to implement the solution to a problem. It is this immediacy of promised benefit that makes problem solving so attractive.

4. We have a general world picture that shows that everything is fine. It will get better through gradual evolution. Maintenance is enough. Anything else is disruptive, risky and liable to upset someone. Complacency is the mood. Do what you are doing and keep doing it. Problems have to be solved because they interfere with maintenance.

It is for all these very good reasons that so many people have come to believe, and have been taught, that thinking is only about problem solving.

Let me make it very clear that I have nothing against problem solving. It is a very valuable and effective part of thinking. I have no intention whatever of indicating that there is anything wrong with problem solving. What I am strongly against is the belief that problem solving is the whole of thinking. That we just have to solve problems and that is all there is to thinking. It is this dominance and exclusiveness that I believe to be dangerous.

In this matter my attitude is exactly the same as it is towards traditional thinking and the contribution of the Gang of Three. I have nothing against critical and analytical thinking. It is excellent and plays a key role in our thinking. But it is only part of the whole process. I am against the belief that it is sufficient.

The analogy I have used before is that the rear wheels of a

car are excellent. I have nothing against them. But they are insufficient.

The other analogy is to do with food. Food is excellent but overeating creates health problems. This is the fault of overeating, not of food. So our obsession with critical thinking and problem solving is not any fault of those processes but of our obsession.

While Western improvement was concerned only with problem solving and putting right the defects, Japanese thinking (uninfluenced by the Gang of Three) was looking at things which were not problems and making things that were good even better in a process of continuous improvement. The West has now been picking up this habit under the framework of 'quality'. But even quality is not enough – we also need creativity. Doing the same thing better and better may not be enough when there is a better thing to do.

In order to show the huge variety of different thinking situations I am now going to go through a list of some of them.

Different Thinking Situations

The following list of different thinking situations is by no means a comprehensive list. Most readers will easily be able to add some situations that I have left out. The purpose of the list is to suggest that the definition of our thinking purpose may be very varied, depending on what we want to do and the type of thinking situation.

In all cases the key question is:

- With what do I want to end up?

A clear answer to that question leads to a definition of the purpose of thinking.

PROBLEM

I am using this in its 'pure' sense. There is a problem. There is a failure. There is a defect. There is a deviation from what should be. Something has gone wrong. Something has broken down. There is pain. There is danger. There is interference with what we would like to be doing. Perhaps there is an obstacle to be overcome. Perhaps there is a gap we have to cross. Perhaps there is something in our way.

In general, there is something that needs to be put right. We would like to be without the problem just as a sick person wants to be without the sickness. We want to remove the interference of the problem. We want to remove the barrier or obstacle of the problem.

The *interference* type problem is somewhat different from the *obstacle* type problem because the first deals with our normal behaviour and the second obstructs a path we want to take. Yet both are interferences we would rather be without.

'*I cannot go away because there is no one to look after the cat.*'

'*My neighbour's loud music prevents my sleeping at night.*'

'*Traffic congestion in cities is becoming appalling.*'

'*Our suppliers have raised their prices.*'

'*The unions are threatening a strike.*'

'*Street crime is rising.*'

- I want to end up with a way of solving this problem.

TASK

A task is something we want to do. We might set the task for ourselves or we might have the task defined for us.

Some people, obsessed with problems, talk about problem finding when they mean setting up a task. A task is something we want to do.

When, as a result of a challenge by a famous mathematician, I set out to invent a simple game, that was a task which I set myself.

Often we are content to survive day to day. Maintenance is enough. We do not set tasks. We do not set bold tasks because they might be difficult to achieve. As we build up confidence in our thinking and our creativity we should become more willing to set bold tasks.

'*I want to learn to speak Chinese.*'

'*I want to make a list of the most creative people in advertising in this town.*'

'*I want to find a way of getting women to drink more beer.*'

'*I want to set up a home for homeless youngsters.*'

'*I want to build the best customer service of any airline.*'

'*I want to find a new way of cooking cabbage.*'

- I want to end up with a way of achieving this task.

ACHIEVE A DREAM

A dream is a special sort of task which happens in your mind or which you gradually fashion. It always seems that a dream, by definition, is out of reach.

If we treat a dream as an excuse to do nothing or to compensate us for something, then the purpose of the dream is not going to be achieved.

But there is no reason why, from time to time, we should not put some thinking effort into achieving that dream.

A friend of mine once had the dream of conducting a Mahler symphony. He was not a musician. But he set about achieving that dream. And he did achieve it. In fact he became a leading conductor of that particular symphony.

'*I have a dream that one day I might become a doctor.*'

'*I dream that I might fit into those slim fashions.*'

'*I have a dream of stepping on to the Centre Court in Wimbledon.*'

'*I have a dream of becoming very rich.*'

- I want to end up with steps towards achieving a dream.

INVENTION

An invention is also a special form of task. The inventor sets out to invent something to carry out some function. There are, however, other aspects.

The inventor needs to find some point where an invention would be needed or be beneficial. Often the most valuable contribution of the inventor is to identify this point. The inventor of the 'Workmate' bench for Black & Decker has received millions in royalties. His contribution was to focus not on the power tools which Black & Decker made so well but on where they were to be used.

There are a number of steps the inventor has to go through.

1. Where and how the invention is going to provide benefit.
2. Figuring out how to do it.
3. Figuring out how to do it in a practical way.
4. Protecting the invention.
5. Putting it into effect or, persuading someone to put it into effect.

All of these can become tasks in their own right. Invention is a classic example of a self-defined task.

- I want to end up with an invention which will carry out this function.

DESIGN

Design is also a form of task. You set out to create something which is not there. It is true that in carrying out the design you may have to overcome certain specified problems (weakness of material, cost, environmental problems, etc.) but the overall purpose is to create something.

You may set the design task for yourself or you may have it given to you as a design brief.

Even in classic problem solving you may need to use design. Where a problem cannot be solved by identifying and removing the cause then you may have to 'design a way forward'.

'*We need to design a way of collecting waste paper.*'

'*We need to design a better parliamentary system.*'

'*I want to design travel wear for business executives.*'

'*I want to design a convention hall that can be used for other purposes as well.*'

'*I want to design a safe toy for very young children.*'

- I want to end up with a design as specified.

IMPROVE IN A DEFINED DIRECTION

'*I want to speed up this process.*'

'*I want to simplify the application forms.*'

'*I want to make this operation safer.*'

'*I want to reduce the energy required for this operation.*'

'*I want to make staff more friendly towards customers.*'

'*I want to strengthen this joint.*'

Where the direction of improvement is actually specified (speed, simplicity, cost reduction, etc.) improvement is a mixture of task, design and even problem solving. Sometimes there is a problem to be overcome; more often things are working reasonably well but we 'believe' that there may be a better way to do things. We then go on to specify what we mean by a 'better' way. There is now a direction towards which we can work. How do I get there? How do we achieve this?

- I want to end up with a way of improving things in the specified direction.

NEGOTIATION

There is thinking which takes place before the negotiation. What do I want to get out of this? What do I hope to achieve? What must I not give way upon?

Then there is the thinking that takes place during the negotiation process.

There is also the thinking that takes place in between negotiation sessions. How far have we got? What do we think of the offer on the table? What is our position now?

There might also be the final stage of presenting the outcome, ensuring compliance, face saving, communication, etc.

There are people who treat negotiation as a problem. How can we overcome this obstacle? How can we get rid of that difficulty?

There are people who regard negotiation as a matter of argument. There are people who regard negotiation as a battle and who seek to apply maximum force.

Then there are people who regard negotiation as a design process. What are the differing positions? What are the differing perceptions? What are the different values, needs and fears? How can we design something that brings these together to give an outcome that is acceptable to both sides (win–win). At this point negotiation becomes a design task.

'*Can we design an outcome that will be acceptable to both sides?*'

'*How do our positions differ on this?*'

'*Given these different fears, how can we design a way to overcome them?*'

'*Let's spell out the values on both sides.*'

'*We are going to have to alter the design.*'

A contract is a form of designed negotiation. Both parties want to move forward, so it is a matter of designing something that covers the values and fears of each side.

There is a form of negotiation in which the two opposing sides never meet. Each side 'designs' the most reasonable outcome for both parties. A judge, or panel, then chooses the most reasonable outcome. There is no argument, no to and fro and no reaction to the proposals of the other side. The emphasis is entirely on the design of the 'most reasonable'. If one party refuses to be reasonable then the other party's proposal is accepted. If both parties seek to be reasonable it probably does not matter which proposal is actually accepted.

The new emphasis on ADR (Alternative Dispute Resolution) seeks to take matters out of the adversarial courts and into the design area.

- I want to end up with an outcome that is acceptable to both sides.

GET THIS INFORMATION

The purpose of the thinking here is to obtain some specified information. In a sense, it becomes an 'information task'. How do we get the information that is required?

The information required may be obtainable with a market survey, as in market research. There may be value in an opinion poll. It may be a matter of asking around. Creativity may be involved in seeking out the information.

Any detective investigating a case has an *information task*. Who committed the crime? What is the evidence? In getting towards this specific information need the detective may, however, go through a phase of 'open' information search. What information, of any sort, can I get?

In this type of thinking it is important to keep in mind that the specific purpose of the thinking is to get the information. What is then done with the information is not part of the defined purpose of the thinking.

'*How do we find out who reads these books?*'

'*We need information on drug dealers in this area.*'

'*What is the business climate in Hungary?*'

'*We need information on related patents in this area.*'

'*We need information on the environmental effects of this herbicide.*'

- I want to end up with the specified information.

CARRY OUT A TASK

This is not the same as specifying a task and then thinking out how to get there, how to carry out the task. In this case the task and way of doing it have been specified. It is a matter of carrying it through.

Why is there any thinking required in carrying out a specified task? If the task is routine or has been specified in great detail then the thinking required may be limited to problems as they arise. But if the task has been specified in broad terms and is not routine then you will need to sit down and to think how you are going to carry out the task.

The thinking may involve organization: which things to do first. The thinking may involve looking for a better or simpler way of doing something. The thinking may involve finding a way of doing something which has only been specified as an objective.

'*How do we arrange this product launch on November 21st in London?*'

'*What would be the simplest way of visiting every hardware store in this area?*'

'*How do I arrange the seating plan for this dinner? Some people will not want to be seated together.*'

'*It is my task to do the school run on Wednesday. What is the best way to do it?*'

'*The recipe is quite clear. But the end result is not what I expected. How can I do it right?*'

- I want to end up with an effective way of carrying out the specified task.

PLAN

Setting out plans is an important part of thinking in its own right. Anything complex requires plans. There may be long-term plans for the future or plans for the next school holidays. There may even be plans for one evening. There may be plans to build a vast theme park. For this there may be the architect's plans and eventually the contractor's plans, which have to be concerned with such details as delivery of the concrete when needed.

Planning requires a lot of projection thinking – looking into the future and anticipating what might go wrong. Running the plans through and seeing what happens. There is also a great need for information. Organization thinking is essential.

Planning also comes in as part of many other types of thinking. You may have to plan how to carry out a task even when the method has been decided. You may have to plan how to implement the solution to a problem. You may have to plan how to proceed with a new creative idea.

Planning is based on steps and on time. What are the steps and when are they going to take place?

'*How do we plan this move to the new site?*'

'*How do we plan the demonstration against the new road?*'

'*How do we plan to bring this garden under control?*'

'*How do we plan to bring in the voters from the outlying places?*'

'*How do we plan the schedule for the summer school?*'

'*How do you plan to take over that company?*'

'How do we plan this expedition?'

- I want to end up with a plan to . . .

ORGANIZE

There is a great deal of overlap between 'plan' and 'organize' because planning is really a special case of organizing.

The characteristic of *organizing* thinking is that all the pieces are there. There are not the unknowns that there might be in creative thinking, in problem solving and in task achieving. How are we going to put these pieces together in the best way?

We could try out every possible way of putting things together and then choose the best. This would take far too long. So we set up 'tasks' and 'constraints', and then try to work with these in order to simplify the task.

As with planning there is a need for a lot of *projectiving* thinking. We have to imagine and visualize what might happen with each suggested proposal.

There is usually a need to have a clear picture of priorities. Is the priority to get as many people into the car park as possible or to allow a speedy exit from the car park?

While the purpose of the thinking at this particular moment may be to carry out the organization, it is also to keep in mind the 'purpose' of the organization.

For example, in a supermarket it might make sense to have

all shelves clearly labelled and food distributed in a way that required minimum walking on the part of the customer. But research shows that something like 80 per cent of supermarket purchases (in the USA) are impulse purchases. So if the way is not clearly signed and if customers walk around then they will buy more.

On the other hand, good organization of the checkout process will make customers more inclined to shop in your store. The same would hold for the car park.

'*How do we organize the Christmas office party?*'

'*The organization of baggage handling at the airport needs some attention.*'

'*How do we organize the book displays in this bookshop?*'

'*The filing system needs organizing differently.*'

'*With these new automatic welders, how do we reorganize the production line?*'

- I want to end up with a way of organizing this.

CHOICE

The alternatives may be presented to you and you have to make a choice. You have to choose between the dishes offered on the menu in a restaurant. You may have to choose between two job offers. You may have to choose between the available colours of a car you want to buy. You may have to choose between two ardent suitors.

At other times you yourself set up the alternatives and then have to choose between them. In such cases always be careful to design several alternatives. Do not just be content with the obvious ones that come first to mind. The creative generation of alternatives is a very important part of the choice process.

Choice is an important part of the overall thinking process. The generative (**PO**) stage produces alternatives and the **SO** stage has to choose between them. Right now we are looking at *things situations* where *choice* is the primary purpose of the thinking.

There is a need for projection and looking into the future with regard to each of the choices. There is a need for the evaluative thinking to be found in the Yellow and Black Hats. There is a need for a clear sense of needs, values and priorities. What is the choice supposed to achieve?

'*We need to choose between these two holiday destinations.*'

'*We need to choose a colour to paint the walls of this room.*'

'*We need to choose between these two designs for the company logo.*'

'*You have to choose which toy you want.*'

'*We have to choose between these two applicants for our new marketing director.*'

'*You need to choose the day for the announcement.*'

Choice brings us back from the realm of 'possibilities' to the actuality of our daily life and needs.

- I want to end up with a definite choice between these alternatives.

DECISION

Decision is a form of choice or choice is a form of decision. Much the same sort of thinking is needed. In the case of decision, however, the need to make the decision and the need to make the decision now is an important factor. We need to think through whether not making the decision is itself a form of decision.

In general, choices tend to affect us but decisions tend to affect other people. This impression is not logically supported and it is easy to find choices that affect others and decisions that only affect ourselves.

Choices tend to be between alternatives; decisions are often concerned with whether to go in a certain direction or not to go in that direction.

As with choices, the priorities, the values, the purpose of the decision and the consequences all need to be examined.

'*We must make a decision about whether to close this plant or not.*'

'*We must decide on a guest list for the wedding.*'

'*Do we accept this offer?*'

'*Does anyone here want to go water skiing this afternoon?*'

'*Have we decided to go ahead with this new advertising campaign?*'

'*Have we yet made a decision on this plan?*'

'*Are we going to sell the house?*'

With decisions it is important to be clear about the decision basis so that, in future, when you doubt the wisdom of the decision, you can refer back to the reasons for making the decision at the time.

- I want to end up with a decision on this matter.

JUDGE

'*I need to judge this.*'

'*We need to assess this proposal.*'

'*Is this an epidemic or is it not?*'

'*Should we raise prices?*'

'*Do you think that was deliberate?*'

'*Did she do a good job as headmistress?*'

'*What do you think of this season's fashions?*'

'*How does it taste?*'

'*Is this wine drinkable?*'

Judgement is a very broad thinking operation. Like choice and decision, judgement comes into the **SO** stage of thinking. We judge the output from the **PO** stage and decide what to do with it: accept, develop or put aside (for the moment or for ever). Judgement is also a thinking situation in its own right.

Judgement can mean recognition and identification. Is this really an epidemic? Is this really legionnaires' disease? In such cases there are characteristics and criteria which will help us to decide. Are these characteristics present?

Then there is judgement which is a matter of assessment. Sometimes this assessment is a matter of opinion but rests on firm principles. Is this legal? At other times the assessment is much more subjective. Is she doing a good job? Is this design attractive? In such subjective assessment there are usually five bands:

1. No doubt at all: it is bad, awful and to be rejected
2. A lot of things against it
3. Neutral: adequate
4. Good things about it
5. Definitely fine and wonderful and to be chosen.

There is also the judgement, which takes place under the Black and Yellow Hats, where we make an effort to pick out the difficulties or the benefits. Here the judgement is itemized. In the end we look at the list and make an overall judgement.

There is judgement involved in a decision whether to do something or not. This takes into account the consequences of action or of inaction.

Judgement can be objective and based on the facts or it can also be subjective and based on feeling (as in the Red Hat) and opinion. Will this person fit in with the group?

Judgement does not actually make the decision. Judgement offers up a judgement. This judgement then plays a part in the decision that is to be made.

- I want to end up with a judgement on this matter.

COMMUNICATE

When communication is obvious or routine then we do not need to do much thinking about it. Too often, perhaps, we assume it to be obvious.

How something is communicated can make a very big difference. A communication may be confusing, unclear and muddled. This may cause real problems or at least require a lot of effort on the part of the receivers of the communication to figure things out. Tax forms can be a classic example here. So are instructions with regards to using electronic equipment. Generally, such instructions are very badly written because they are written by people who know the device and to whom everything is therefore obvious. It is a different matter for those who have just bought the device.

Poor communication can give the wrong impression and cause damage and mischief. Good communication should not only avoid giving the wrong impression but should also seek to counter the wrong impressions that some people might have.

Communication should also give the impression of being simple, direct, honest and sincere.

This is a task involving design and creativity. Sometimes there are specific problems to be overcome.

'*How do we tell the workers about the proposed lay-offs?*'

'*How do we tell him he has failed the exam?*'

'*There is something really new here. How do we communicate it?*'

'*How do we communicate the health risks involved in smoking?*'

'How do we lay out the instructions on how to use this new toaster?'

'How do we communicate that he is leaving his post because he has been asked to resign?'

- I want to end up with a good way to communicate this.

EXPLORE

This is a very common and a very broad type of thinking purpose. You simply want to explore an area. You do not have a purpose other than to find out more about the area. Sometimes you may have another more specific purpose at the back of your mind but for the moment you are just exploring.

Exploring and the collection of information is what takes place in the **LO** stage of thinking. But exploration can be the whole purpose of the thinking. An explorer who lands on the moon or explores a remote part of Papua New Guinea has the purpose of finding out more.

As soon as you permit yourself a background purpose to the exploration you reduce the value of the exploration as such, because now you only notice things that might be of value to your background purpose. Genuine exploration is interested in what is there – not in what suits your purpose.

'I want information about walking holidays in France.'

'I want to explore the possibilities of doing business in China.'

'Please look into the area of fish-farming in cold waters.'

'Explore the whole area of creativity.'

'*Find out about provincial art dealers.*'

A previous *thinking situation* described earlier covered a request to obtain specific information. This was a sort of task to be carried out. Exploration is very much broader. We want all the information in a field. Obviously, the field does have to be specified because you could not ask for all the information about everything. The definition of the field may be so narrow that the difference between 'explore' and an 'information task' may be small. In practice, exploration is open-ended and does not specify what you are going to find. An information task defines what you are to look for.

- I want to end up with a thorough exploration of this area.

GENERAL IMPROVEMENT

An earlier 'thinking situation' described improvement in a defined direction: making something faster, simpler, cheaper, etc. Here improvement is general. We just want improvement but do not specify the direction and do not know in what direction it is to come.

Obviously, it would be possible to treat general improvement as a series of specific improvements. We could set out some defined directions and then seek to make improvements in each of them. This would end up as a series of problem-solving exercises.

General improvement is more creative and more open-ended. We do not exactly know with what we are going to end up. The improvement might lie in a direction we would never have thought of and could not have defined. Beer drinking amongst women went up when the quality of the toilets in pubs was improved. No marketing man would have suggested this as a way of getting women to drink beer.

General improvement follows a belief that whatever is being done is not necessarily the best way of doing it. Rather than treat it as a problem the matter is treated as a creative exercise. What ideas can we have here? The ideas are then examined to see how, where and if they offer improvement. The ideas comes first.

'*How can we make mealtimes more interesting?*'

'*How can we improve newspapers?*'

'*Improve the news programmes on TV.*'

'*Improve the appearance of cars.*'

'*Improve supermarket displays.*'

'*I want to improve the uniforms of police officers.*'

'*I want ideas to improve this dishwasher.*'

'*Improve communication in the home.*'

- I want to end up with any sort of improvement in the defined area.

OPPORTUNITY

Most people have been told that any problem can be turned into an opportunity. But we remain much more interested in problem solving than in opportunity seeking. Very few people actually sit down to think about opportunities. If an opportunity stares us in the face then we might assess it, but this is not the same as actively seeking opportunities.

This real lack of interest in opportunities probably arises from two sources. Opportunity means risk, bother and hassle, and we do not like any of these. We have also adapted to the way things are and are content with the way things are. There is little motivation to change.

Businesses are supposed to be out there seeking opportunities the whole time. In my experience this is not so. Businesses are more interested in creativity for solving problems than for finding opportunities.

We can look for opportunities or we can design them. We can start from our strengths and assets, and see how these might be used. Or we can start from the market and the world, and see what opportunities are opening up. In practice we would probably start from both ends.

Seeking opportunities is open-ended. We do not know where we are going to end up. If we have a specific task then that becomes a task: 'How can we sell confectionery in the former Soviet Union?' The opportunity might have been defined as: 'Where else can we sell confectionery?' or 'What else can we do with our capacity to produce confectionery?'

In seeking opportunities we often need some frameworks for directing attention. I laid out a number of such frameworks in my book *Opportunities*.*

**Opportunities*, Penguin Books, 1978.

- I want to end up with some opportunity possibilities (in this area).

CHANGE (THINK ABOUT IT)

Something has changed: in the world, in the market or in the regulations. We want to think about that change. How does it affect us? What opportunities are opened up?

We usually think about change only if it creates a problem for us or obviously affects us directly. Here the thinking purpose is a deliberate exploration of change. The emphasis is on opportunities. Any change is potentially a source of opportunity for those who spot the opportunity first. After a change things are not the same as they were before the change.

No one is forced to think about change in this open-ended way. But you can 'choose' to think about change in this way.

'*What are the effects of this change?*'

'*What opportunities are opened up by the new regulations?*'

'*How does the opening of the Channel Tunnel affect our travel plans?*'

'*The electrification of the rail line to this place is going to cause some changes. How can we benefit from those changes?*'

'*Big companies are laying off people. What opportunities does that create for us?*'

'*NAFTA (North American Free Trade Association) has now been set up. Let's think about it.*'

'*The children have all left school. What does that lead to?*'

- I want to end up with some ideas arising from this change.

PEACE, EXCITEMENT OR HAPPINESS

We can set out to think about peace or excitement or happiness. Usually we seek to obtain these or increase our enjoyment of them. We may also seek to inject more of them into our daily lives.

This is thinking which involves both task and design. There may also be problem solving if we are conscious of barriers which stand between us and these desired objectives.

What is characteristic about this type of thinking is that the objective or destination is very broad indeed. It is very difficult to aim at 'happiness'. We might think of various situations or things that could make us happy and then we assess those situations to see whether they will in fact deliver happiness.

There is no harm in thinking about such broad objectives. What will happen is that you will generate possibilities and then will need to work on these and finally assess them.

'*I want to think about happiness.*'

'*I want more excitement in my life.*'

'*I want to find more peace.*'

'*Why am I not more happy?*'

- I want to end up with ideas in the area of happiness (peace, excitement, etc.).

COPE WITH CHANGE

This is not the same as the exploration of change mentioned earlier. Here it is a matter of adapting to change and coping with change which does affect you or the organization directly. Some of the difficulties and problems may be obvious. Others emerge only over time. There has been a disruption. The old equilibrium is no more. It may be a matter of damage limitation.

We can anticipate some of the effects of change. We can set up structures to cope better with change. All this requires thinking, as does the response to unforeseen difficulties that arise.

This sort of thinking is adaptive thinking, which may include specific problems. There is a large component of design thinking. There will also be a need for creative thinking. Planning is often involved. Keeping your balance on a surfboard is a matter of continuous adjustment. There is no one stance which makes subsequent adjustment unnecessary.

'*How are we going to cope with this new competitive threat?*'

'*Retirement is a big change. We have to adjust to it.*'

'*Being out of a job is a big change. We have to think about how we are going to cope.*'

'*This back injury means that I am going to have to learn a new job.*'

'*The huge importation of cheap toys from China has hit us very hard.*'

'*The market has changed. There are no longer lots of small outlets, only a few big outlets, and if you cannot get into these you are finished. So they can squeeze you on margins.*'

- I want to end up with a strategy for coping with this change.

FORMULATE A DREAM

If a dream has been formulated, then it is a matter of 'task thinking' to reach towards that dream. But where does the dream come from? How is the dream formulated?

It is a legitimate purpose of thinking to set about formulating a dream or a bold task. The difficulty is to avoid reducing the dream in order to make it more reachable. On the other hand, if the dream remains totally vague and unformed then it might serve as a dream but not as something you might ever achieve. You may wish to formulate a dream that is not a dream to be reached but one to cheer you up and keep you going. This is a design choice.

Formulating a dream is similar to designing a task or formulating a design brief. Put in what you want to be there.

'*I want to think about a dream life-style.*'

'*I want to pin down the characteristics of the ideal business for me.*'

'*What do I want out of life?*'

'*What do I expect marriage to be like?*'

'*Who is the dream customer?*'

'*What is the ideal place to live? What characteristics would it have?*'

- I want to end up with a well-constructed dream (task or design brief).

INITIATIVE

We can go through life reacting to problems and opportunities as they arise – or we can take initiatives from time to time.

Sometimes young people set off with great courage to a distant land. They do not know exactly what they are going to do when they get there. They survive and sometimes they succeed.

Initiatives require some courage but they need not require a great deal of courage. You can think through an initiative in order to minimize the risk. You can prepare a 'fall-back position' in case the initiative does not work. Initiatives usually do require hard work because you cannot just float along in the usual 'maintenance' way. Sometimes with an initiative you have to take your own steps all the way. At other times the initiative is to switch to another channel and then get carried along in that new channel.

You may want to take an initiative because nothing else is happening. You may want to take an initiative because you are bored with what you are doing. You may want to take an initiative because there is some attraction that beckons you forward. Sometimes you may have a very precise sense of where you are going and the initiative becomes a detailed plan. At other times you take the initiative and then see what happens. You then think again in order to go forward.

'*If you want to get a job you are going to have to take some initiatives.*'

'*Nothing much is happening – we must try some initiatives.*'

'*The market is very quiet. What initiatives can we take?*'

'*Sitting at home is not going to get you to meet more people. You need to take some initiative.*'

'*Let's design some initiatives here.*'

● I want to end up with some initiatives.

OUTCOME, REVIEW AND SUMMARY

At the end of the **SO** stage of thinking there should be a conclusion, an outcome or summary. So producing an outcome is part of every thinking process. Even if the outcome states that 'there is no agreement on this matter and no practical steps forward have been found', that is still an outcome and may be a very good summary.

There are also times when the whole purpose of the thinking is to produce an outcome. The purpose of the meeting may be to put down the outcome of a meeting, a discussion or a stage in an ongoing process. The thinking required may be complex. There is a need to cover all the ground and yet to reduce the matter to a few essentials. It is a sort of process of distillation.

Sometimes there really is no outcome, so the thinking is directed towards bringing about an outcome. This becomes a task or design process.

Review thinking is of this type. Periodically you may want to sit down to review a situation. What is going on? What has been achieved? What are the changes? What are the problems? What is likely to happen next?

'*What is the outcome of the thinking we have been doing over these last few weeks?*'

'*I want to try to put all our decisions together into one comprehensive outcome.*'

'*What would you say is the outcome of our discussion?*'

'*We ought to review where we are at the moment.*'

'Could you prepare a review of our investments in the Far East?'

'Let's summarize what we have been thinking about.'

- I want to end up with an outcome (summary, review).

NEUTRAL-AREA FOCUS

This is almost the exact opposite of problem solving or task achieving. We have no idea where we are going to end up. We have no idea why we are even thinking about this matter at all. Yet it is a very important part of thinking.

We tend only to think about matters where there is some obvious benefit to be derived from the thinking. That is why problem solving is so appealing. With a task we perceive benefit if the task is achieved.

With neutral-area thinking we just focus arbitrarily on an area and decide to think about it. We do not know if we are going to derive any benefit from the thinking. We use creativity to generate new ideas in this neutral area. We then scan these ideas for potential benefit and if we see benefit we seek to develop ideas into usable ideas.

Many things continue as they are because they have never been problems and have therefore never attracted thinking attention. Inventors often benefit from thinking about things other people have never bothered to think about.

You can choose to think about the point on a pencil that is three inches from the writing end. Why? Because you want to. No other reason at all. You can choose to focus on where you write the date on a cheque. Why? Because you want to.

If you do not get any great ideas, then all you have lost is a little thinking time. But you have practised your creative thinking skills and also helped develop the habit of stopping to think about anything and everything.

'*I want to think about the shape of traffic-lights.*'

'*I want to think about the way a cup sits on a saucer.*'

'*I want to think about how interest is paid on a bank loan.*'

'*I want to think about newspaper headlines.*'

'*Let's give some creative attention to seats on buses.*'

'*Let's think about discounts in supermarkets.*'

- I want to end up with some new ideas in this specific area.

BLANK-SHEET CREATIVITY

In some ways this is similar to neutral-area focus. There is no problem. There is no task. There are no visible benefits to be obtained. You have a 'blank sheet' of paper and you are asked to be creative.

It may be designing a new logo or writing a pop song or inventing a new child's toy.

It is not strictly correct to say that there is no purpose because the purpose of both neutral-area focus and blank-sheet creativity is to come up with valuable new ideas. That is certainly a purpose – but a general background purpose. There is no specific design brief.

The real difference between blank-sheet creativity and neutral-area focus is that with blank-sheet creativity you are specifically requested to come up with ideas. And you really do start with a blank sheet. With neutral-area focus you choose the focus yourself and there is focus even if there is no reason for choosing it. In both cases the creativity is totally open-ended. Later we shall consider some creative techniques for working in such open-ended situations.

'*I want a totally new idea for a perfume bottle.*'

'*Think of a present for someone who has everything.*'

'*Design a new merit award.*'

'*What shall we call the new puppy?*'

'*Design a new adult game.*'

'*I want some really new idea for the sales of chewing-gum.*'

'*Let's design a new banking service.*'

- I want to end up with some new ideas that serve the specified purpose.

EXPLANATION

You look to find out why something has happened or why it is happening. You might be looking for the cause of a problem. You might be looking for a basic scientific principle or phenomenon. You might be a detective investigating a crime. You might be unravelling a fraud. You might be a young man wondering why his girlfriend has left him.

There is information to be gathered. There are guesses or hypotheses to be made. You collect some information. You make a hypothesis and then you collect further information to support or reject that hypothesis. In science you devise experiments. The trick is to make good use of hypotheses but to avoid being trapped by them, so that you only see what the hypothesis allows you to see.

'*What happened here?*'

'*We are trying to find out who committed this crime.*'

'*Why are more young women than young men starting to smoke?*'

'*What is the explanation of this overheating at this joint?*'

'*How did that shipment get lost?*'

'*What made her behave like that?*'

- I want to end up with an explanation of this.

LOOKING INTO THE FUTURE

There are people whose job it is to look into the future. People want to know the changes, the opportunities and the threats. If you are involved in long-term planning then you need to have some idea of what the world is going to be like long term. Other people also want to look into the future in order to make decisions.

Many things can be extended from the present or from present trends. Babies alive today will grow up. Children will grow up. Trends towards increasing automation at work will continue. People will become more affluent. There will be more cars on the roads. People will travel more. We can look at today and say this will increase or that will decrease. We can even say that two things might come together to create a third.

There are also *discontinuities* or things which are not extensions of today. We have to use creativity in order to imagine these discontinuities. You can never prove that they are going to happen. They can only remain as possibilities. But by thinking of them now we become ready to see them when and if they arrive.

'*What will work be like in twenty years' time?*'

'*Will cities continue to grow?*'

'*Will our children want to go on living in this big house?*'

'*What about the environment in the future?*'

'*Will there be nuclear fusion in fifty years' time?*'

'*What about China and India as industrial nations?*'

- I want to end up with a clear picture of the future.

CRISIS

The main thing about crisis thinking is the time pressure. There is a need to do something.

Crisis thinking requires a clear assessment of what is going on – and the ability to change that assessment as things progress. There is a need for decision-making and a clear line of command. Priorities are very important because it often becomes a matter of giving up something in order to save something else. All the time there is a need to create options. There is also a need to project and to imagine what might happen next. Problem solving is involved but it is usually not easy to remove the cause of the problem. Designing a way forward may be more important.

'The water supply has been contaminated, what do we do?'

'John has been involved in a bad car accident.'

'The computer has crashed.'

'The gunmen are holding two hostages inside the bank.'

'The guests have arrived but the wine has not.'

'Mary has run out of money in the middle of India.'

- I want to end up with a way of coping with this crisis.

STRATEGY

A strategy is not as detailed as a plan. It is more a set of guidelines. Later these will need to be put into a plan. The point is that the guidelines remain but the plans may vary with the situation. The way you implement a strategy may vary while the strategy remains constant.

Sam Walton's strategy was to take organized shopping to smaller towns where there was little competition. As a result he built up the largest retail chain in the USA and became one of the richest Americans. A politician might have a strategy of always being helpful and offering to do the things which no one else wanted to do.

In putting together a strategy there is consideration of strengths, weaknesses, opportunities and what the world is going to be like. A big corporation might say that it is too difficult to foresee the future therefore the strategy is to do nothing but wait for things to emerge and then to be very quick in moving with the trends.

'What is our strategy for winning this game?'

'We need a strategy for entering this new market.'

'Could you spell out the strategy we are following?'

'This election needs a definite strategy.'

'We should sell off the operations that require a lot of attention but have no future.'

'What is your strategy for finding a job?'

- I want to end up with a defined strategy.

CREATIVE THINKING

Creative thinking comes into very many of the situations described here. For example creative thinking is demanded in the 'blank-sheet' situation or the 'neutral focus'. In design, task achievement, negotiation and problem solving, creative thinking is also required. Creativity is one of the key ingredients of thinking. Its purpose is to create new ideas and fresh options.

There are also times when we decide that we want to do some specific creative thinking about a focus, a situation, a task or a problem. The emphasis now is not just on solving the problem or having some adequate ideas. The emphasis is on 'new ideas' which have not been mentioned before.

Once the new ideas have been 'created' then they can be examined, improved, assessed and, occasionally, used. The deliberate use of creativity is based on the belief that the existing ideas may not be the only ones or the best ones.

'We need some new ideas for holidays.'

'Can we have some more creative cooking?'

'We must develop a more creative approach to the youth market.'

'I want some new ideas for the book cover.'

'We are going to repaint that room. Do you have any creative ideas?'

'The competition from the big stores is killing us. We need a special creative approach.'

- I want to end up with some fresh creative ideas.

General Summary

The list of thinking situations given here is by no means complete. My intention has been to show a wide range of situations. For each situation there is a desired output: 'I want to end up with . . .' You do need to be very clear as to what you want. It is not good enough to feel, vaguely, that you are thinking about a certain matter.

Readers will have noticed that all the situations can really be treated as two fundamental types of focus:

1. *Area* focus
2. *Purpose* focus.

1. AREA FOCUS

With area focus we simply define where we are starting. We want some new ideas 'in this area'. Pure examples of this would be *blank-sheet thinking* and *neutral-area focus*. We just define where we are thinking. The overall purpose is, of course, to produce useful ideas, but there is never a defined task to be achieved or problem to be solved. Opportunity thinking can be an area focus; so can *general improvement*. Exploration is a form of area focus.

Area focus is important for two reasons. Area focus allows us to think about anything at all. Without area focus we should be restricted to thinking about problems and defects. The second advantage of area focus is that our thinking is not limited by our existing ideas. Whenever we have a 'purpose' we are in fact limiting our thinking to that purpose. With area focus the thinking is totally free.

2. PURPOSE FOCUS

This is the more traditional 'thinking for a purpose'. We want to solve the problem. We want to achieve the defined task. We want to end up with a plan. We want to make an improvement in a defined direction. With purpose focus we know where we want to be in rather specific terms. 'I want to stop the leak from the roof' is very different from 'I want some new ideas about roofs.'

Summary of the TO Stage

Time spent thinking about the 'purpose' of your thinking is time well spent. Be very clear about this purpose and spell it out. Change it, redefine it, try alternatives, broaden or narrow it – but be clear about what you finally decide to think towards. The word 'to' symbolizes: 'Where am I going to?'

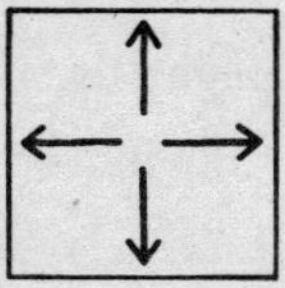

LO

The Information Stage

Lo and behold
Lo / ok
Lay **O**ut

The symbol for the **LO** stage of thinking shows arrows pointing in four directions. We look around in all directions. The **LO** stage is to do with gathering in information as the background and basis for our thinking.

It would be very simple to write: 'Gather as much information as you can.' That would then be the end of this section. Unfortunately, it is rather more complicated than that.

This **LO** stage corresponds to the white hat in the Six Hats framework. This is the hat concerned with gathering information.

In the CoRT Thinking Programme there is a whole section devoted to information and feeling (CoRT 5). Many of the perceptual tools from CoRT 1 are also useful in the **LO** stage. These include:

CAF Consider All Factors
C&S Consequences and Sequels
OPV Other People's Views.

Thinking is no substitute for information. Instead of thinking what time the last plane from London to Paris might fly, it would be better to consult a timetable or phone for information.

Is Information Enough?

There are times when the whole purpose of our thinking is to obtain the information we need. We need to think where we can get the information and how reliable the information will be. We also need information in order to start thinking where we might find the information.

We have come to believe that information may be enough and that collecting more and more information will do all our thinking for us. This belief is based on the habits established by the Gang of Three and is also encouraged by school and university. There was a time when all useful information could be taught. So schools and universities saw it as their job to teach this information. Those days are long gone but schools and universities have not changed much. Information is easy to teach and easy to test.

Socrates believed that 'knowledge was all' and if you but had the knowledge then choice and action were obvious and easy. On holiday you set out to drive across the island you are visiting. If you had a road map it would be easier to find your way. If you knew the road map was reliable and up-to-date then your task would be even easier. If a resident then told you about the nature of each of the alternative roads, the traffic conditions, the view, etc., then your choice of route would be very easy indeed. Of course, you would apply your own values to the information. Do you want the scenic route or do you want to get to the other side of the island as quickly as possible? In this case information and values are enough. There is not much thinking to be done. There are many situations where good information is enough and makes thinking unnecessary or very easy. So our thinking is best directed towards how we get the information.

From Aristotle came the *box* or category type of thinking. A child with a rash is seen by the doctor. What is the diagnosis? The doctor looks through her mind to find the boxes which are labelled 'common rashes in children'. Perhaps it is sunburn. Perhaps it is an allergy. Perhaps it is measles. Each of these conditions has its own box with a set of characteristics. The doctor judges the characteristics shown by the child against each box. Is there a fever? Sunburn or allergy would not normally give a fever. So the doctor chooses the 'measles' box and makes the diagnosis. Action is then easy because the treatment of measles is also written on the outside of the box.

So the system is easy. We derive 'boxes' from collective experience and also personal experience. When we come across something we judge which box the something fits into – then the action is determined by pre-set patterns of dealing with that box. This *recognition* system works very well indeed because the boxes are set up over time by learned people but everyone else can then use them. Each person does not have to set up boxes for himself or herself. Education passes on the boxes. Life is made simple.

It is true that the system has two key dangers. The first danger is that of stereotyping and prejudice, which leads to racism and ethnic conflicts. The second danger is that the boxes derived from the past may be inadequate to deal with a changed world.

Nevertheless, the system works well. So attempts at identification or recognition can be part of the **LO** stage. Usually some strong feature suggests a group of possible 'boxes'; each of these is then checked out against the situation using all the characteristics of each box. An apple does not go into the orange box just because it is round; we check out the colour, the finer shape and the nature of the peel – also the smell.

When we set out to solve a problem we try to get as much information as possible. We seek to identify the cause of the problem. Then we can solve the problem by removing the cause.

It is therefore quite true that there are times when information alone will do our thinking for us. But it is a mistake to believe that more and more information will always make thinking unnecessary. Later in this section I shall indicate why information is not always enough.

Sources of Information

The most used source is our own mind. That means personal experience, the residue of what we have been taught in formal education and what we have picked up over the years from friends, books and the media.

Today with on-line computer systems and excellent libraries it is possible to get access to a huge amount of information.

Learning how to access such systems and what to look for now becomes very important. There is no shortage of technical information. Much of this is not much help in personal thinking matters. Suppose research showed that, on average, women were more truthful than men. Would this research help you? Not much, because it does not mean that the particular woman you are dealing with is truthful or that if a woman and man are involved that the woman is telling the truth and the man lying. Statistical research is not much help with individual cases.

Questions

Questions have always been the classic way of obtaining information from other people. We can also use questions to obtain information from ourselves or to direct our search for information. This is the basis of so-called Socratic questions, although Socrates mainly asked his listener to agree with what had been said. A question is a device for directing attention, as I indicated earlier: 'Direct your attention to this matter and tell me what you find.'

There are two broad types of questions (described in the CoRT programme):

1. Fishing questions
2. Shooting questions.

FISHING QUESTIONS

When we go fishing we put the bait in the water and do not really know what is going to turn up. A fishing question is open-ended.

'How many people came to the party?'

'What substance would resist corrosion?'

'What are the agricultural exports of China?'

SHOOTING QUESTIONS

When we go shooting we aim at something in particular. We do not shoot up into the air and hope that a bird might be passing. So shooting questions have a known aim. They are checking-out questions. We already have something in mind and want to check it out.

'Were there more than twenty people at the party last night?'

'Will aluminium resist corrosion in fresh water?'

'Have the agricultural exports of China increased in the last five years?'

The answer to a shooting question is always 'yes' or 'no'. You hit the target or you do not.

Skilful questioning involves a combination of both fishing questions and shooting questions.

Quality of Information

There are facts which can be checked again and again. There are authority figures who should know what they are saying. There are general opinions which most people seem to hold. There are things which are 'known', although you yourself have never checked them out. There are the opinions of people who are regarded by some as authorities but by others as unreliable.

In general, we prefer to stick to the facts and try to exclude all else. This is a mistake. We should acknowledge all sorts of information but at the same time label the information with its perceived quality. You can acknowledge that a rumour exists but do not have to believe the rumour. You can accept that an opinion exists but do not have to agree with it. We need to develop the habit of mind that records information just as a camera records a scene.

- There is this poor-quality information . . .
- There is this high-quality information . . .

Sometimes you may need to ask questions in order to determine the quality of the information: 'Why do you say that?' It is not a matter of disagreeing and arguing that something is wrong but a matter of exploring the basis for the information that is offered.

Perception

Perception is an extremely important part of thinking. We have largely neglected this important part of thinking for a number of reasons:

1. We have been so obsessed with the truth and checkable facts that we have rejected perception, which is subjective and uncheckable.

2. There is no right and wrong about perception. Perception is valid for the person holding that perception.

3. The subjectivity of perception was emphasized by the

Sophists, and Plato wanted to get rid of that and move to absolutes, which were not subjective.

- What are our perceptions?
- What are the perceptions of the other people involved?

Whether we like it or not, perceptions are a reality. Perception is the way we look at the world or the way our minds organize what we are seeing at this moment. If people have a perception that one shop is better value than another this is what will guide their buying behaviour – even if the facts show otherwise. Facts can be used to seek to change perceptions but in the end people can only act on their individual perceptions. If people perceive that one politician is more dishonest and self-seeking than another, then that is how they will vote. The underlying truth is irrelevant.

It is no use claiming that a perception is faulty and can therefore be ignored. A perception is a reality whether it is correct or faulty.

When thinking about a subject we often need to broaden our own perceptions. Are we taking too narrow a view? Have we left something out of consideration? Just 'wanting' to broaden your perception is some help but is usually not effective enough. That is why the CoRT Thinking Programme introduces some very simple *attention-directing tools*.

What factors should we take into account when designing a chair? What factors should we take into account when planning a holiday? What factors should we take into account when buying a new car? What factors should we take into account when appointing a new marketing manager? The simple CAF tools ask students to Consider All Factors. An eight-year-old in a rural black school in South Africa can apply this to 'buying a new cow' just as easily as a sophisticated executive could apply it to redesigning a computer network.

Considering the consequences of an action is very much part of the evaluation process (the **SO** stage of thinking). But paying some attention to known consequences is also part of the **LO** stage. A doctor prescribing a medicine needs to be conscious of the possible side-effects. The C&S tool from the CoRT programme requests specific attention to the consequences and sequels to an action. Where these are known they are part of the information input.

Most thinking involves other people. So our perception needs to take these other people into account. Indeed, our perception needs to take into account the different perceptions of other people. The OPV tool from the CoRT lessons directs attention to Other People's Views. How do other people see the situation? How do smokers see a ban on smoking in restaurants? How do non-smokers see this ban? How do restaurant owners see it? How do restaurant staff see it? Politicians are always having to take into account the views and perceptions of other people.

It is not the purpose of the **LO** stage of thinking to seek to change perceptions. The effort is to note what the perceptions actually are or what they might possibly be if you cannot ascertain what they are.

Feelings

There is a notion that feelings are subjective and messy and should therefore play no part in objective logical thinking. This is totally absurd. Feelings exist and do play a large part in our thinking. In the end, it is our feelings which give any value to the outcome of our thinking. The purpose of thinking is to serve our values and our feelings. This is not to say that feelings are always helpful or justified. That is a different matter. But feelings exist and should therefore be attended to and noted in the **LO** stage of thinking.

- What are my feelings about this matter?
- What are the feelings of the other people involved?

In the Six Hats framework the red hat specifically requests individuals to express their feelings on the matter at this moment in time. Feelings are acknowledged as one of the ingredients. If one member of the family does not like that colour of car this may not affect the final choice but it is an ingredient.

Once again, it is not the role of the **LO** stage to argue about feelings and to seek to change them. It is enough to record the feelings.

Analysis

Analysis is an active effort to produce recognition and to produce more information.

It is difficult to deal with complex matters so we seek to break them down into smaller parts which are easier to deal with. Sometimes, this breaking-down procedure produces parts which we can now recognize. We may end up seeing the complex matter as being made up of parts with which we are very familiar. So now we think we understand the matter. Without analysis understanding would be very difficult because we can only understand something in terms of what we already know.

Analysis is a sort of attention-directing framework. In its simplest form analysis means breaking something down into its component parts. We may 'decompose' a bicycle into its parts: wheels, frame, handlebars, chain, pedals, etc. These are the parts which would have been put together to make up the bicycle.

We could also analyse the factors that made a bicycle attractive. Here we would have to depend much more on perception. There would be items like robustness, ease of repair, comfort, ease of mounting, safety, weather resistance, likelihood of theft, fashion, price, image, etc. All these are much more intangible than wheels and pedals.

Economists would seek to analyse the factors involved in inflation: money supply; velocity of money; inflation expectations; printing of money; channelling of money; too few goods and services; no competitive pressures, etc. They would disagree on the factors that mattered. They would disagree on how the factors interacted. They would disagree on where intervention was possible. Nevertheless, it would be very difficult to do anything about inflation without first analysing the process.

Usually universities are very good at encouraging the habits of analysis. The trouble is that they do not encourage much else.

The Search for Information

It is easy enough to say 'Get all the information you can.' In some cases there is far too much information. There are 33,000 medical journals published every year. Scientific information doubles every few years. How do we direct the search for information?

There are three basic types of information:

1. What you know
2. What you know you do not know
3. What you do not know that you do not know.

The first type is easy. It is the knowledge you have. The second type is more difficult. How do we know what we need? How do we define the information that we should have?

A detective first sets out to get all the information available. Then she forms a guess, a possibility or a hypothesis. This hypothesis now directs the search for further information. Where was the suspect on the night in question? Does the DNA of the bloodstains match that of the suspect? What possible motive might there have been? In a way the initial 'fishing questions' are now followed by a series of 'shooting questions'.

There may be a continuous flow from information to hypothesis and then back to more information; then a change in the hypothesis and then more information, etc. This is also how science works.

So there are three stages:

1. Some general information
2. Hypothesis and more information
3. Seeking to challenge the hypothesis.

Hypotheses are immensely useful and we could not begin to think without them. They can be as formal as a scientific hypothesis or as simple as a 'guess'. They serve to direct our search for information. There is, however, the danger that we can become trapped within a hypothesis. We end up seeing only what the hypothesis wants us to see. We are oblivious to the rest. So in the end we need to challenge the hypothesis and to seek to try other hypotheses.

When the roof is leaking you 'guess' that a drainpipe is blocked so you direct your search for information to the drainpipes. When an electric lamp will not light you guess that it might be the bulb or the fuse so you direct attention to these. We make these guesses all the time. We would not be able to do anything without such guesses. The guesses can be wrong. In the story of the alarm clock in Pasadena I guessed that it was the hotel alarm clock which was making the noise and so proceeded to try to shut it up. My guess was wrong because it was my own alarm clock.

The ability to form hypotheses is the very essence of science.

The analysis of data is only a service to the checking out of hypotheses. Yet most of the emphasis in the teaching of science is on the analysis of data, not on the formation of hypotheses. This is because it is assumed that it is easy to form hypotheses. It is not. Forming hypotheses requires creativity and the understanding of a wide range of processes.

Sometimes the underlying hypothesis need not be obvious when we 'define the gap' in the information that we have. It may be that an obvious piece of information is missing. For example, when there has been a fall in sales we would like to know whether there had been a price change or whether a competitor had just launched a competing product. Most of the time we can define a gap because we have some reason (a hypothesis) for supposing the missing information to be useful. For instance we might want to know what has happened to the sales of competing products. The hypothesis is that all products of this type have falling sales. We might want to know if the fall in sales has been sudden or gradual. The hypothesis is that a sudden fall might have been due to adverse publicity at some point. The better we are at defining the gap in our information the more useful will be the information we collect.

We come now to the third situation: what we do not know that we do not know. It is easy enough to seek out information that we know we should have. But how do you search for information when you are not even aware of the possibility of its existence? There are two possible approaches to this very difficult problem.

The first approach is to conceive of even remote possibilities and then to search in that direction – even if you do not have much hope of success.

The second approach is to expose yourself to some *random* information in the field. If you always look only for what you are looking for then you will stay within your existing ideas. Opening yourself up to some random input allows you to move outside these boundaries. This may mean going to exhibitions of other professions, reading magazines you would not normally select and speaking to people from different fields. The success of cross-disciplinary research arises exactly from the need to be exposed to things for which you could not have looked because you could not have imagined the possibility of their existing.

Making the Most of the Information

In a famous Sherlock Holmes story the most significant point is that the 'dog did not bark in the night'. It was this absence of barking which was significant, because it suggested that the murderer must have been known to the dog.

I have often read an article in a magazine and then talked to someone who has read exactly the same article. Yet I seem to be telling that person things which were available in the article. This is not just a matter of a better memory. Most people read without really trying to extract the full significance of what is being offered. The writer usually has a story line or message. Very often the most important information has nothing to do with this story line or message. If you just follow the story line then you miss the other information. It is true that you cannot see the other information unless you already have in your mind some frameworks or ideas which give significance to the information. But if you have been thinking about the subject at all then you should have a mind rich in such frameworks.

You read that certain categories of crime have decreased. Your mind should start thinking of possibilities:

'*Are people less inclined to commit crime?*'

'*Are the police doing a better job?*'

'*Are people not reporting certain types of crime because nothing ever happens when they do report it?*'

'*Has the classification system of crime been changed?*'

As you read the rest of the report you may now notice information which supports one or other of these possibilities.

Reading between the lines and seeking to extract the full 'inferences' from the information is hard work but it can become a habit. You then find that you are stocking your mind with information that can be useful in many different places.

A model is a more elaborate form of a hypothesis. You may have a mental model of the economy or of a cell membrane. You construct the model to fit in with the known data. Then you run the model, in your mind or on a computer, and see what happens. This gives you a better understanding of what might be going on. It also allows you to make predictions and then check out these predictions. The model works this way –

let us see if the real world behaves in the same way. The model provides information but we have constructed that model. The model will also suggest how we can influence the system. Then we try this out and see if it works.

You can never prove that your model is the actual one or the only possible one. At best you can say that the model is compatible with all we know about the subject and that the model provides useful results. Another model might do the same. It was a model of how the neural networks in the brain work as a self-organizing information system that gave rise to the formal techniques of lateral thinking. These were then shown to work in their own right. Their value arises from their practical 'use value' but their origin was in the model.

Information is Not Enough

We return now to the point that was discussed at the beginning of this section. In many cases information is enough and will do our thinking for us. But there are times when this is not so and when the belief that it is so can be limiting.

When most people enter a new field, in research or in business, they want to read all they can about this new field. They want to absorb all the information first and then to start to do their own thinking. This is a very natural thing to do but it could be wrong.

When you have read all the information that is available from the experts in the field then your mind will be forced to use the concepts and perceptions that are traditional in that field.

It will be extremely difficult to generate new ideas. It is true that you can challenge the existing ideas and set off in an opposite direction. But it is virtually impossible to have a slightly different idea because you will immediately be pulled back into the channel of the traditional idea.

So what is the alternative? Can we really think usefully about a field if we do not know the field at all?

We can start out to read something about the field. Just enough to give us a 'feel' for the field. Just enough to sense the 'idiom' of the field. Then we stop and do our own creative thinking. We think up new concepts, new perceptions and new ways of doing things. Then we go back and read some more. Then we stop again to do our own thinking. Finally we go back and read all there is to read. In this way we are seeing the field through some of our own ideas. There is therefore much more chance of developing fresh ideas. This is the creativity of innocence.

There is a widespread belief that if you analyse information, this will give you new ideas. This is not so. Analysing information will allow you to select from the standard ideas you already have in mind. You might even combine some of these standard ideas. But you will not 'see' a new idea. The mind can only 'see' what it is prepared to see. Therefore you need to start the idea in your mind as a speculation, a guess, a possibility or a hypothesis. Then you look at the data through this guess and see if the data supports the guess.

It is true that neural-network computers will pick out patterns in data but this will not tell you the basis for these patterns.

Sometimes this does not matter. Supposing the computer tells you that people who own dogs buy more insurance. If you are selling insurance, you then know that it is worth targeting dog owners.

In business people use a lot of market research to seek to predict whether a new product will succeed. Market research provides good information about *what is* but not about *what might be*. Market research always looks backwards even if the questions are framed to look forwards. When bank customers were asked if they would like to get money from a 'machine' they mostly indicated that they much preferred a human teller. But once the machines (ATMs) were installed and customers had got used to them, they then found they much preferred the machines to the human tellers. Queues would form at the machines when the tellers were not busy. Within Japan the Japanese do not use much market research – they prefer to try things out and then to let the market decide. It is very difficult for a person to say how they would react to something which they have not yet experienced.

In an early book, *The Five-day Course in Thinking*, I set out some problems with knives and bottles. I said that four knives could be used. The first problem only required three knives for the solution. I got a great number of very angry letters asking why I had said that four knives could be used when actually only three were required. In problems set at school we are so used to being given only the information that we need for that problem that we actually leave school believing that life will carefully lay out the information we need in every situation. Unfortunately, life does not do that. There are times when we might have to put aside some information in order to move forwards. This requires thinking.

So although there are times when information alone is enough there are also other times when more and more information will not do our thinking for us. We need creativity, hypotheses and the putting together of information in design.

Summary of the LO Stage

In the second or **LO** stage of thinking we set out to gather information, perceptions and feelings. This provides the basis and also the ingredients for the thinking that is to follow.

Sometimes we need to direct our search for information with guesses or hypotheses. We should record the information but also note the quality of the information.

There are times when more information will do our thinking for us. There are times when more information will not do our thinking for us and we need to develop ideas, possibilities and designs.

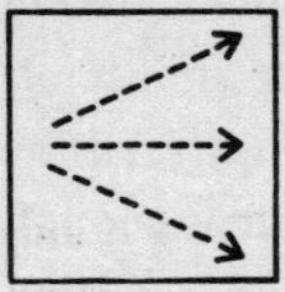

PO

What are the Possibilities?

Possible
Potential
Sup**po**se
Hy**po**thesis
Poetry

The symbol for the **PO** stage of thinking shows three arrows heading forward. The three arrows suggest multiple possibilities. The purpose of the **PO** stage is to produce multiple possibilities for achieving what we want from the thinking. These possibilities are then fed into the **SO** stage, which develops, evaluates and selects from amongst these possibilities. The broken lines of the arrows in the symbol indicate that these are only 'possibilities'. In the **PO** stage we open up possibilities. They have not yet been confirmed, checked out or converted into lines of action or choice.

PO and Possibility

Many years ago I invented the new word *po* as a formal indication that a provocation was to follow. A provocation is a statement that we know to be wrong but which we use in order to jerk us out of our usual thinking so that we can form new ideas. This **PO** stage of thinking takes the broader use of the word to cover 'possibility' as well.

As I have stated earlier the *possibility system* is an extremely important part of thinking. It is responsible for almost all progress and certainly for the great progress of Western civilization in science and technology. Sadly, it is very much neglected in education, which pretends that progress is a matter of analysis and logic. Any understanding of how the brain works would indicate that analysis and logic must be inadequate for moving ahead of our information. But the traditions of the Gang of Three, reinforced by ecclesiastical and legal argument habits, have enforced this obsession with what is at best a limited form of thinking.

In science, possibility provides the speculative guesses that we call hypotheses. In technology, possibility provides the dreams and visions which we can then work towards (such as a plane that flies faster than sound or a computer on a thumbnail).

All the words used at the beginning of this section (possible, potential, hypothesis, suppose, poetry) have a 'forward effect'. We use these words to move 'forward'. We make such statements in order to see what they lead to (the process of 'movement'). In poetry we put together words and images in order to see what effect we have produced. All this is very different from 'prose', which is an attempt at describing 'what is'. Prose is concerned with *what is* but poetry is concerned with *what can be*.

Our official traditional dislike of the 'possibility' system arises from a misunderstanding of its nature. The possibility system opened up any number of strange myths and beliefs for which there was no proof. There is no limit on this fertile process. People then came to believe these myths as 'true'. So the 'scientific method' and 'logic' came along to insist that you should only accept as true what could be 'proved'. As a result the possibility system was thrown out. At its worst the possibility system insisted that you had to believe something unless you could absolutely disprove it. You have to believe in little green men from Mars landing on the earth unless you could disprove that possibility.

It was this mistaking of 'possibility' for 'truth' that caused the trouble. Possibility is not truth and should never pretend to be. Possibility is a framework in the mind that makes it easier for us to move forward to what might be the truth. That is precisely how a hypothesis works in science. Even if we temporarily believe something to be true we can still move forward with a hypothesis to a fuller truth. Einstein moved forward from Newtonian physics, which had been perfectly adequate up to that point.

The supporters of the possibility system need to be clear that possibility is not truth. The opponents of the possibility system need to realize that the process is an essential part of the dynamics of any thinking that is not simply descriptive.

Possibility is always creative. Possibility always moves forward from 'what is'. The possibility system falls under the green hat in the Six Hats framework. Under the green hat we seek to put forward new ideas, further alternatives, modifications of the idea, possibilities and provocations.

The creative section of the CoRT Thinking Programme is CoRT 4. This includes the deliberate and formal tools of creativity which will be described later in this section.

Three Levels of Possibility

We need to be clear about three different levels of possibility. It is when we confuse these levels that we get into trouble. The three levels are:

1. Possibility
2. Fantasy
3. Provocation.

Imagine that you are standing on the top of a burning building. Consider three levels of possibility.

1. It is possible that the fire-engines are on the way. It is possible that you might be rescued by ladder or even by helicopter.
2. It is a fantasy to believe that Superman will swoop out of the sky to rescue you or that someone will sprinkle fairy dust on you and enable you to fly to safety.
3. It is a provocation to say 'Po the building might melt down and deposit you on the ground.' The point about a provocation is that you do not believe it at all but merely use it to *move forward* to a practical idea – are there any parts of the building which might collapse gradually?

Making the Connection

The **TO** stage of thinking will have established where we want to get to. The purpose of our thinking at this moment should be clearly established.

The **LO** stage of thinking will have clearly established where we are at the present. This includes the information we have, the perceptions and the feelings that exist around the matter.

So how do we make the 'connection' between where we are and where we want to be?

You can call this connecting 'problem solving', 'creative achievement', 'design' and any number of other things. Far too often we treat it all as 'problem solving', which is limiting and dangerous.

I intend to simplify the process into four basic methods. These methods do overlap and there can be a large number of variations of each method. It seems to me, however, that these are the four fundamental approaches.

At the end of the **PO** stage we should have some possibilities. These are then fed into the **SO** stage which takes these possibilities, develops and evaluates them, and finally decides on one practical way forward.

The **PO** stage is the generative, productive and creative stage of thinking.

The Four Basic Approaches

1. The search for standard or routine solutions. These solutions are available to us and we search our minds to find the appropriate solution or way forward.

2. Here we move from a very general statement of what we

need to a specific solution. We can also use general statements to work backwards from where we want to be to where we are.

3. This is the creative approach. We deliberately create new ideas and then seek to modify them to suit our purposes.

4. This is the design or assembly approach. We put together different elements to achieve the desired purpose. These elements may be obtained from standard sources or through creativity.

There are thinking situations where one or other of the four approaches is clearly the most appropriate. For example in 'blank-sheet' thinking, where you are asked to come up with new ideas, then the creative approach is appropriate, whereas the routine one is not. Where the thinking purpose is to obtain information then the routine approach might be better than the creative approach. Sometimes all four approaches can be tried on the same situation.

At all times the thinker needs to keep in mind what he or she is really looking for.

1. Are you looking for *any* solution which will get you to where you want to be? There are times when any solution is enough. You just want to get on with things.

2. Are you looking for a *good* solution? This means a solution that fits your needs; is not expensive in time, money or effort; and is attractive. So you may wish to move beyond the first 'adequate' solution that comes to mind to find another one.

3. Are you looking for a *better* solution? You are really looking for the *best*, but accept that it would be presumptuous to suppose that one solution was the 'best'. Here you have adequate solutions that you could use but you keep on looking for a better solution. You may want one which is new and creative. You may want one which does more than just fit your needs and has some 'plus' to it. If you do not find this 'better' solution you can always go back and use the adequate solution that you know about.

We can now consider each of the four approaches to making the connection between where we are and where we want to be.

1. The Search for the Routine

This is by far the most used method. The routine response to the situation may be obvious. In that case not much thinking is required. If the response is not so obvious then we have to do some thinking in order to find the routine response.

You want to know how to get from London to Paris in the afternoon. The way of finding the information is routine. You look up the airline timetable. You phone your travel agent. Does any thinking come into it? You may have to think which method is easiest at this moment in time. Your information or **LO** stage is also important. If you have heard about the Channel Tunnel then you might think of asking your travel agent about this. Looking into an airline timetable will not tell you anything about the tunnel. A routine which was once appropriate (flying) may no longer be so appropriate.

The traditional *box* system set up by Aristotle precisely fills this routine-response purpose. We seek to identify the situation. Once we have done that then the action has already been worked out and is attached to the appropriate 'box'. There is a box called measles. As soon as the doctor can put the illness into that box then the treatment is routine and standard. This recognition and identification does require thinking. What are the main features? What group of boxes should we be looking at? What preliminary guess, speculation or hypothesis can we make which might direct our search?

When we think we have identified the situation (found the right box) then we still have to do a lot of thinking. How good is the match? How can we get the information we need to confirm the match? What are the features that go against this match? What other possibilities might there be?

The whole of the legal system is based on this search for routines. The routines are the principles laid down by the legal codes, in countries where law is codified, or by precedent where law is built up by precedents. There are now comprehensive computer systems which allow a lawyer to search extensively for past responses.

In court there are then two types of argument. The first is whether the accused has or has not committed the crime. This is an argued judgement as to whether the accused falls into the *guilty box* or the *innocent box*. Evidence is put forward and argued about. There is an attempt to find the 'truth'. The second type of argument is to decide which 'box' the action fits into. The boxes are laws, principles, prior judgements, etc. Which principle is relevant? Do we have a case of this or of that? Which law is to be applied here? It can get confusing when different principles or laws all seem to be applicable. The judge then seeks for some finer dicrimination as the basis for judgement. In the end the judgement is of the nature 'this is in this box'. In some countries tricky judgements can set a precedent which makes it easier for future judges dealing with similar cases. A new box has been set up.

Psychologists love creating categories, types, personality clusters, etc. She is type A. He is type B. This is not difficult to do. You set up questionnaires and gradually pick out those questions which discriminate between groups best. The next step is much more difficult. What does it mean? What is the usefulness? The danger arises when we give general titles to these boxes, such as 'intelligence' or 'judgemental' or 'innovative'. We then come to believe the general meaning of those words. So everyone in the intelligence box is intelligent and those outside are not. Does the box cover all that we might mean by intelligence or only that type of intelligence which has actually been tested by a particular test? Then we come to the usefulness of the boxes. Suppose that we can show that at a certain age men are better at mathematics than women are. Does this mean that if I want a good mathematician I should only look to employ a man? That would be total rubbish since the overlap would be huge. Does it mean that we should not bother to teach much mathematics to women? On the contrary, it now seems that where a difference has existed it is because of the poor teaching of mathematics to women. Does it mean that if you find yourself in one box then you should try to get out of it? If you are firmly in the 'feeling' box then you should try to develop some thinking as well. There is value in this, except that classification in the first case may have made you see yourself so firmly in that box that you come to prefer feeling over thinking. So the effect may even be counter-productive.

English people only pick and eat classic mushrooms because they are so terrified of picking poisonous toadstools. French people pick and eat a huge variety of mushrooms because they have become expert at a much finer discrimination. They have many more mushroom 'boxes' to play with. A wine expert or a perfume 'nose' has developed a great number of 'boxes', so that taste and smell can be categorized in a much more detailed way.

The dangers of categorization and stereotyping have already been mentioned. If you believe the generalization that all Scotsmen are mean then you are on the lookout for this and if your dining companion hesitates slightly in offering to share the bill you immediately bring your stereotype into play. Racial and ethnic problems arise from the ease of categorization, which both allows myths to build up and also makes them easy to apply.

For most cases the search for routines is the most valuable thinking method. You need to turn a screw? So find a screwdriver.

Analysis

In complex situations there is often no box available. Sometimes a box does get created. Inflation is a complex matter with many factors involved. But current economic thinking has decided that inflation can be put in one box and that the treatment is raising the interest rates to reduce the money supply. This has now become standard *box* thinking and no government dares be different. The result is that the treatment of inflation can cause severe economic recession. What is then treating the inflation is not the restriction of the money supply but recession as such. But no government would dare use recession as an economic tool.

Analysis is our tool for breaking down complex situations into small parts. These smaller parts are easier to recognize. In fact we go on breaking something down into parts small enough for us to deal with.

We analyse 'juvenile' crime and come to the conclusion that lack of employment is a factor. This is now a familiar box. So we seek to create jobs for youth.

We analyse the problem of traffic congestion in cities and come to the conclusion that motorists find it too easy and convenient to drive into cities. We then move to the standard response: make it difficult and inconvenient. So we restrict parking and tow cars away, or we charge motorists for driving into the city centre, as in Singapore.

The purpose of analysis is to break things down to the point where standard responses can be applied. With regard to human affairs the standard responses are incredibly limited – to 'reward' (incentives) or 'punishment' (discouragement). It is believed that the careful application of these two standard responses will control all human behaviour.

On the whole our analysis thinking can be very good because

that is what education has been all about. But the standard responses are usually limited, poor and primitive because we have given so little attention to 'design'. We have believed that analysis can take us to the stage where simplistic responses are enough. This is one of the major faults of our current thinking systems.

In conflicts like that in Bosnia Herzegovina the standard responses are limited to: 'Do we hit the Serbs harder or do we not.'

Similarity

Analysis is one way of treating a situation so that we can end up with matter for which standard responses are available. Another way is similarity: 'This is similar to . . .'

Would-be politicians are advised to study history. When a situation arises you then say to yourself: 'This is like the situation facing Metternich at such and such a time' or 'It seems to me we are in the Stanley Baldwin situation dealing with the abdication of Edward VIII.' This provides a frame for thinking about the situation and even suggestions as to the most appropriate actions. Unfortunately times change and history may be as much a trap as a help.

Again the preference is for identifying a classic 'box' because this will then determine action. This preference is easy to understand. We know from particular history or accumulated history that these standard responses have worked. So if we correctly identify the box and apply the standard response then we are sure of success. That is how a doctor treats measles or a streptococcal sore throat. The alternative to standard-box response is to 'design' the appropriate action. But there is no guarantee at all that this designed action will work. It is little wonder that we prefer to search for routine solutions.

In personal relationships we use *similarity* all the time. A person reminds us of someone we used to know and so we believe we can understand that person's feelings and motivation and can predict his or her actions.

Transform the Problem

Mathematicians are said to work by setting out to transform any problem they come across into one they know how to deal with. This is a very sensible strategy. We use it all the time in order to apply the 'search for routine' type of thinking. Analysis and similarity are ways of transforming the problem into one we know how to deal with. We can also set out to transform the problem directly through redefining it.

With the story about the slow lifts the problem was transformed into one of 'impatience'. How do we deal with impatience? Give people something to do. So we install mirrors around the entrances to the lifts and people occupy themselves in looking at themselves and others in the mirrors.

THREE THINKING SITUATIONS

I intend to illustrate the four different thinking approaches by applying each of the approaches to a set of three thinking needs. These have been chosen so that all four processes can be applied. It would not be much use choosing a purely creative need and then seeking to apply routine thinking.

SITUATION A The car park is too small and people coming in to work complain that they cannot get into the car park.

Routine Search Response If something is in short supply ration it or auction it. So limit the number of those who have a right to use the car park. Or auction the use on a 'first come, first served' basis. Those who get up early get the use of the car park. Maybe they will also start work earlier.

- We could seek to transform the problem by shifting it to the users. Let them form a committee to come up with suggestions about use of the car park.

SITUATION B Someone has opened a new restaurant. The owner wants to get business moving as fast as possible. What could the owner do?

Routine Search Response People will recognize value, so give good food at reasonable prices and in time you will build up a clientele. If people hear about your restaurant they will tend to come, so employ a publicity agent.

- We could transform the problem to one of providing cash flow to begin with. So set up a catering service and even home meal deliveries to provide revenue.

SITUATION C There is a certain wall in the middle of town which seems to be a great temptation to graffiti writers. The wall is always covered with ugly graffiti. What can be done?

Routine Search Response Deter the offenders. Catch some of those doing the graffiti and punish them by making them scrub off the graffiti for some weeks.

- We could transform the problem from preventing the writing of graffiti to preventing the permanence of the graffiti. This suggests the new non-stick surface on which it is impossible to write.

2. The 'General' Approach

In the basic thinking processes I discussed earlier in the book I emphasized the huge importance of being able to work at the *general*, *broad* or *blurry* level. This is exactly the approach that we shall now be examining. Skilled thinkers and skilled problem solvers use this approach the whole time. I would almost go so far as to say that those who show a natural thinking aptitude do so for two reasons: their ability to think on a 'general' level and their ability to 'project'.

Thinking in general terms means thinking on a concept level. Some people are very impatient and unhappy with conceptual thinking. They believe conceptual thinking to be academic, airy-fairy and playing around. They want practical, hands-on advice. What do I do now? What do I do in this situation? They want routines. They want routines that they can use in the 'search for routines' type of thinking. Americans are particularly impatient with concepts. They want action. As a pioneer nation action was always more important than thinking. Today thinking is more important than action – and they feel uncomfortable with concepts and with thinking.

The 'search for routines' and the 'general' approach are not totally separate. In the end what we do will often be some routine. We can also use concepts in order to search for a routine – as in the examples on pages 144–5. The main difference is in the start of the thinking.

'*I have to loosen this screw. I need a screwdriver.*'

That would be the routine approach.

'*I have to loosen this screw. I need something which can fit into the screw and that can be turned.*'

If a screwdriver was to hand you would use the screwdriver but if there was no screwdriver you would also think of using a knife, a nail-file or even the edge of a credit card.

So having established the purpose of our thinking we describe what we 'need' in a very general way.

'*I need a way of getting to Paris this afternoon.*'

'*I need a way of blocking the leak from the roof.*'

'*I need a way of making absenteeism more difficult.*'

There are two types of situation:

1. Where we could use a specific routine response but prefer to put it in a more general way. So instead of saying, 'I need to know the airline timetable from London to Paris', you say, 'I need a way of getting from London to Paris.' This more general statement could allow the examination of the Channel Tunnel option.

2. Where there is no specific routine, so we have to put it in a

general sense anyway: 'I need a way of making that table fold up.'

Of course, even our choice of a general concept can channel our thinking into a certain direction. In dealing with absenteeism we might say:

'*I want a way of making absenteeism more difficult.*'

'*I want a way of encouraging people to stay at work.*'

'*I want a way of preventing absenteeism from disrupting the work.*'

'*I want a way of preserving productivity in spite of absenteeism.*'

'*I want a way of giving group responsibility to workers with regard to absenteeism.*'

All of the above could come under the more general terms of:

'*I want a way of reducing absenteeism.*'

'*I want a way of living with absenteeism.*'

The overall purpose of the thinking should then have been defined as 'thinking about the problem of absenteeism'.

We shall return to this particular point when examining the Concept Fan later in this section.

In stating the 'general' need there is no need to be confined to one need. You can express several alternative or parallel needs. This was what was done with the 'absenteeism' problem examined above.

Consider:

'*We need a screwdriver.*'

'*We need a way of turning this screw.*'

'*We need a way of removing the screw.*'

'*We need a way of making the screw ineffective.*'

'*We need a way of separating these pieces.*'

Concepts vary very much in their broadness or generality. At this stage there is no harm in having in parallel concepts which are of different degrees of broadness – even when one concept could be said to include some of the others. In the Concept Fan process the concepts are separated out.

WORKING BACKWARDS

This can be a powerful method of thinking but is not easy to do. In a few cases 'working backwards' can be obvious. I want to go from London to Edinburgh. I know that if only I could get to Newcastle then it is easy to get from there to Edinburgh. But how do I get to Newcastle? Well, if I got to York then it is easy to get to Newcastle from York. But how do I get to York? If I got to Peterborough then it is easy to get to York. How do I get to Peterborough? That is easy enough from London. So the route has been laid out. The problem has been solved.

In some cases we could work methodically. If I got to that point the next step to the destination would be easy. Now that point becomes the destination, how do I get there?

If goods were out of reach, then there could be no shoplifting. But how can goods be out of reach? Put them behind doors which can only be opened with a credit card. Or indicate the goods you want and pick them up at the checkout point.

If shoplifters could easily be caught they would keep away. How can we indicate to shoplifters that they can be caught? Video cameras, rewarding other shoppers for helping to catch shoplifters, publicizing those that have been caught, etc., would all be ways of doing this.

If stolen goods could not be taken from the store there would be no point in stealing them. How can we prevent stolen goods from being taken from the store? Perhaps by giving all goods a scent which would be removed at checkout or be detected by a fierce dog at the entrance.

In a sense 'working backwards' is a form of 'problem shift' or 'problem transformation'.

Working backwards usually requires one or more concept steps, as in the shoplifting example. In a sense the Concept Fan is a form of working backwards. We could reach A from B. Now how do we get to B. From C. So how do we get to C?

We shall go on to consider two other ways of using the 'general' method. Before that, however, we shall apply this first aspect to the three standard thinking situations.

SITUATION A The problem of the limited car-parking space.

'General' Approach We need a bigger car park. This may mean enlarging the car park, building upwards, building downwards or having another park at a distance with a shuttle bus service.

SITUATION B The new restaurant that wants to build up business fast.

'General' Approach People have to know about the restaurant quickly. Engineer a scandal. Hire celebrity look-alikes to dine there. Allow 'topless' dining.

SITUATION C The graffiti problem.

'General' Approach Make the graffiti invisible. Have a curtain that comes down during the day to hide whatever graffiti have been put up during the night.

THE CONCEPT FAN

This is part of the 'general' approach.

On the right-hand side of the page we put down the purpose of our thinking. This must always be an achievement point. There is a problem to be solved. There is a task to be achieved. There is improvement to be made in a specific direction. The Concept Fan does not work with a design or open-ended, creative situation. The destination does need to be defined.

Then we say: what broad concepts (called directions) will get us to this destination. Suppose we were dealing with the problem of a shortage of trained staff. The broad concepts might be:

- Increase the supply of trained staff
- Reduce the need for trained staff
- Get more work out of the staff we have.

Then we take each one of these broad concepts and make it the destination. How do we get there? How do we move in that 'direction'?

So how do we increase the supply of trained staff?

- Recruit trained staff
- Train staff
- Get outside trained staff to do the work (outsourcing).

So how do we reduce the need for trained staff?

- De-skill the jobs
- Automation
- Reduce operations
- Lower standards.

So how do we get more work out of the staff we have?

- Productivity incentives
- Working longer hours
- Using their special skills all the time
- Full use of their time.

Then we take each of the 'concepts' and look around for practical ways to implement that concept. We do this for each concept. The fan now opens out with many alternative ways of tackling the problem. We can take some examples rather than work through each concept.

Concept: train staff.

- *Idea*: train our own staff.
- *Idea*: contract out the work to our own staff who have to acquire their own training.
- *Idea*: set up a training institute in cooperation with others who have the same problem.

Concept: automation.

- *Idea*: use expert systems to make decisions.
- *Idea*: computer-controlled machinery.
- *Idea*: electronic scanning and filing of documents.

Concept: using their special skills all the time.

- *Idea*: give skilled workers personal assistants to do all the work that does not require the special skills.

The two key questions with the Concept Fan are:

1. How does this work? This question takes us towards the broad, concept end of the fan. What is the actual mechanism through which this will work? Why will buses ease the problem of traffic congestion? Because they increase the 'density' of travel: more people per vehicle.

2. How can this be done? This question takes us towards the idea or detail end of the fan. What specific ideas might there be for putting this into practice? How can we implement this concept? How can we reduce peak travel? By staggering working hours. By alerting people to peak times so that they can avoid them.

A point may occur at many different positions in a Concept Fan. For example 'do without' is both a broad direction for coping with a water shortage but also a concept serving the direction of 'reduce consumption'. The Concept Fan is not analytical, so the same point can be repeated as often as you wish.

Concept Fans usually require several editions. You lay out your first fan and then you change and improve it to give the second edition. There may even be a third edition. It is a powerful process but it does need practice.

In the first 'general' approach I indicated that concepts of differing degrees of breadth could be put alongside one another. In the Concept Fan there are levels of concept. The first level is the very broad level or 'direction'. Then come the concepts. Finally there is the practical idea level. Sometimes there may be several levels of concept between 'direction' and 'practical idea'. Each level would be more specific than the preceding level.

We can apply the Concept Fan to the three thinking situations and then proceed on to the third part of the 'general' approach.

SITUATION A The car park problem.

Concept Fan The broad directions might be:

- Increase the car park
- Decrease the size of cars
- Reduce the use of the car park
- Make people happier with the present situation.

We could follow each of these directions but we shall take one of them as an example: how do we make people happier with the present situation?

- We let them decide the use
- We reward them for not using the car park
- We make it a matter of chance
- We provide a better alternative.

We let them set up a committee to decide how to use the car park. We let them vote on alternatives.

We pay them more if they choose to give up their right to the car park. We allow them to come in later if they do not use the car park (or leave earlier).

The right to use the car park is drawn by lot every month. So there is no question of privilege or jealousy.

We make arrangements for car pooling. We buy minibuses for car pooling. We arrange shuttle buses to train stations or other car parks.

SITUATION B The new restaurant situation.

Concept Fan The main directions might be:

- Attract local clientele
- Get repeat customers
- Attract people from afar.

For repeat customers the concepts might include:

- Membership
- Permanent vouchers
- Special privileges.

As ideas to carry out the concept of special privileges we might consider:

- Always being guaranteed a table or a free meal next time
- Naming tables after people
- Discount on the wines
- No tipping
- Right to use premises for parties

Each one of the directions could be pursued and each one of the concepts could be opened out into practical ideas. Only examples have been given here.

SITUATION C The graffiti problem.

Concept Fan The general directions might be:

- Discourage writers
- Make it impossible to write
- Make it easy to clean
- Make the graffiti attractive
- Hide the graffiti.

We can take the broad direction of 'making graffiti attractive'. How might we set about doing this?

- Instruction
- Competition
- Licences.

How might we implement the concept of 'competition'?

- *Idea*: groups compete for the right to use the wall for one week. Their proposed work has to be seen in sketch form first. The best wins the right.
- *Idea*: the wall is divided into areas and individuals compete on a theme – one design per area. The public judge which is the best.
- *Idea*: those who volunteer to clean the wall most often win the right to use the wall for an equal period. So if a group

cleans up the wall for one month then they have the right to use the wall for a month.

In all these examples I have not worked through each Concept Fan in full detail because that would have been tedious for the reader. Concept Fans do take time because they are comprehensive.

One of the great advantages of the Concept Fan is that it gives us several new 'thinking destinations': 'How do I do this?'

There is therefore a cascade effect as each new destination produces a number of alternatives, each of which also becomes a destination to produce further alternatives.

THE 'SOMETHING' APPROACH – MAGIC WORDS

This is obviously part of the general approach.

'*We need something to open this lock.*'

'*We need some way of deterring shoplifters.*'

'*We need something to strengthen this strut.*'

'*We need something to encourage people to vote.*'

'*We need something to measure out toothpaste.*'

We define what the something needs to do. We may define it in a very general way or we may be very precise.

'*We need some way of producing the book you want to read on a stand beside your favourite chair, with proper lighting, without any effort on your part.'*

If we could find this then people might read books as readily as they watch television.

At this point I intend to put some 'magic' into thinking.

Imagine a 'magic substance' which could do anything that you told it to do. I am going to pour this magic substance on the roof. It will find the cracks and seal them so that the roof will not leak any more. I am going to put this magic substance on to goods in the supermarket so that if they are not checked out, a dog at the entrance can pounce on the thief. This magic substance would be automatically cancelled by the checkout procedure. Once we have defined exactly what the magic substance will do, then we set out to find something or design something that will do these things. Is there a scent which could be cancelled by ultraviolet light at the checkout point? Could we design such a scent? Perhaps we do not cancel the scent but add another one to mask it?

There are no limits on magic. So you can require the magic substance to do anything at all. These requirements do not have to be reasonable or practical. You may or may not be able to find some practical substance to do what the magic one has been asked to do. But you will open up ideas and possibilities.

Instead of having to say 'magic substance' each time we can condense this idea into a new word.

The word is *pomat*. This stands for 'po-matter', which indicates magic matter which can do anything you want it to do.

'*We need some pomat to change the colour of the cup according to the temperature of the coffee.*'

'*We need some pomat to mark cars that jump the red lights.*'

'*We need some pomat to stick spaghetti together so we can sell spaghetti balls.*'

'*We need some pomat to coat car windscreens so the water does not obscure our vision.*'

Of course, not everything can be solved with a magic substance. Sometimes we need a 'magic system'. This is a system in which everything will happen exactly as we want it to happen.

So we create a word to indicate this magic system. The word is *posys*, which stands for 'po-system'.

'*We need a posys which will discriminate between regular shoppers and occasional shoppers.*'

'*We need a posys that will increase the penalty for a crime if that crime becomes more relevant.*'

'*We need a posys which will give a much stronger role to the opposition in a democracy. This posys will allow them to get legislation passed if there is support for it amongst the population.*'

'*We need a posys to take care of routine shopping so we do not have to bother about it.*'

Next we come to 'people'. There are times when we need 'magic people' who are going to do exactly what we want them to do. Such people are neither matter nor systems – so we need a word for these magic people.

The new word is *pobod*, which stands for 'pobody'.

'*We need a pobod who can mix entertainment and teaching in just the right amount.*'

'*We need pobods who become caricatures when serving in the restaurant.*'

'*We need pobods who do not mind doing routine things day after day.*'

'*I need a pobod who wants to be a permanent number two and never wants to be number one.*'

'*This pobod can tell at once if a person is being dishonest.*'

Then there are ideal or magical situations in which everything and everyone functions exactly as you would want them to function.

For this magical situation we can create the word *postat*, which stands for 'po-state'.

'*I would like to see a postat in which everyone benefited from our success.*'

'*It would be nice to have a postat in which everyone was working constructively towards a solution.*'

'*We need a postat in which people become aware that environmental damage now will hurt their children later.*'

'*In this postat people exchange their services on a trust basis. There is no money and no cheating.*'

At first the use of these new magic words will seem awkward and artificial. At first a reader may feel that he or she can do just as well without them. And that will be true. Until you get used to the words you will simply be using them to substitute for ordinary words. It is only when you become comfortable with their use that you will find yourself able to do things that otherwise might be awkward or even impossible.

Let us now return to the three thinking situations.

SITUATION A The car park problem.

We need some pomat that would shrink cars to a small size when they entered the car park. This might suggest offering guaranteed parking to motor cycles and bicycles. It might suggest offering the free use of motor scooters for those who needed mobility during the day. It might mean giving smaller cars a greater chance in a lottery to determine car park users.

SITUATION B The new restaurant and building up business.

We need a posys in which anyone who used the restaurant would automatically advertise it to other people. We might give out special scarves or fake fur hats to diners so that other people could notice them. These items might have a very individual colour such as orange or purple.

SITUATION C The graffiti problem.

I want a pobod who sits by the wall constantly and frightens people away. This might lead to the idea of video cameras placed high up. There might be a security light when people got close to the wall. There might be a tape-recorded message which was activated when contact was made with the wall. There might be the sound of police sirens, etc.

We have now come to the end of the 'general' approach, which has been considered under three separate headings. There is considerable overlap between the three parts of the approach.

The main point about the 'general' approach is that we state our needs in a very general way. Then we seek to get more specific. Far too many people limit their thinking because they have been taught that you need to be specific and precise at every point in your thinking. If you believe this then you can never use the power of the general approach. You can never look precisely at something if you do not know where it is. You can look in the general direction and then gradually narrow down your search.

3. The Creative Approach

It is obvious that when we want 'new' ideas the 'search for routine' approach will not do.

In open-ended creativity, such as when we start from a 'blank sheet' or from a 'neutral focus', there is no defined end point. We just want new ideas. So the general approach will not work either because there are no needs that can be requested in a 'general' sense. The Concept Fan, for example, only works when there is something definite to be achieved.

The creative approach is essential when we know where we are starting (area focus) but do not know where we are going to end up. We want to end up with ideas that are new and usable but they may be of any form. They may be beyond what we could have looked for in the first place. In such cases the creative approach is essential. There is no other way we could proceed.

The creative approach is also useful in all other situations even when there is a defined problem or task to be achieved. We may fail to obtain a solution from the other methods. Or we may obtain a solution but are not content with it and want to go on to find a better solution.

During any approach we may stop and say to ourselves: we need some new ideas here; we need some fresh alternatives. We then seek to apply creative thinking precisely at that point. For example, in doing a Concept Fan on 'traffic congestion in cities' we may develop the concept of 'rewarding those who choose to leave their cars at home'. There are no standard routine ways of doing this, so we define this as a new focus and apply some creative thinking to finding ways of rewarding motorists for leaving their cars at home.

THE CHALLENGE PROCESS

This is the simplest form of creativity but it can require a lot of discipline.

In the 'challenge process' you direct your attention to anything at all. You can focus on the point of a pencil or on a point halfway along the pencil. You can focus on the colour of the pencil, the width, the length, the material, etc., etc. You then 'challenge' the way it is usually done:

There are three basic questions:

1. Do we need to do this at all?
2. Why is it done this way?
3. What other ways of doing it might there be?

Sometimes we can go straight to the third question.

Challenge is never an attack or a criticism. This is a very important point. If you use challenge as a criticism then you will only be able to challenge where you see fault. This limits the challenge process very much. You must be able to challenge anything. If you use challenge as a criticism then someone will defend what you are challenging and you will spend your time arguing the point.

Challenge says: '*This may well be the best way of doing it. This may be the only way of doing it. But I want to spend some time exploring for other ways.*'

When, and if, other ways are found, then those other ways will be examined and compared to the existing way.

Challenge is really a habit of mind and an attitude of mind. Challenge can be used on an everyday basis. Challenge can be used during any of the other **PO** stage processes. At any point you can 'challenge' something: does it have to be this way?

Outer World

Challenge can be used on things in the outer world. You can challenge objects or parts of objects. You can also challenge systems or parts of systems. You can challenge situations or parts of situations. Sometimes what you challenge may be very small and inconspicuous. You can challenge the way you start undoing a zip. You can challenge the placement of the date on a cheque. You can challenge the shape of traffic-lights. You can challenge the way the pages in a book are numbered from 1 to the end. (Why not have them numbered downwards so the last page is 1 – then you can tell how much more there is to read?)

The skill of *challenge* lies in:

1. Picking out the focus point to be challenged
2. Applying the challenge process properly
3. Your ability to devise alternatives.

Inner World

Just as we can challenge things in the outer world, we can also challenge things in the 'inner world'. This means we can challenge things in our 'current thinking'. This may be your current thinking, the current thinking of the group you are working with, the current thinking of your company or the current thinking of everyone within that sector or industry.

- Why do we think of things this way?
- Why do we have to think of things like this?

We can challenge assumptions. We can challenge the boundaries within which we think we have to work. We can challenge the ideas that dominate our thinking. We can challenge the values we use. We can challenge concepts. We can challenge the polarizations we make. We can challenge the things we normally seek and the things we normally avoid.

Challenge means: *'Let's stop and think about this. Does it have to be this way?'*

The Use of 'Challenge'

We can spell out our normal approach to a problem or our normal way of carrying out a task. This normal approach may come from the 'search for routine' method or from the 'general' method.

- How would we normally approach this?
- How would we normally do this?

We then challenge the whole approach or parts of it:

'*Do the bank money machines have to be accessible at all times?*'

'*Do we need to have the food on shelves in the supermarket?*'

'*Does a cheque need a date on it?*'

'*Do traffic-lights have to be visible?*'

'*Do we need to worry about abuse?*'

'*Do we need a scheme which will cover all the unemployed?*'

The challenge may free us from boundaries or assumptions that are not really necessary. The challenge may suggest alternatives.

Challenge can also be applied directly to a 'neutral-area focus'. For example, we might focus on the middle of a pencil.

'*Why does it have to be the same shape as the rest of the pencil?*'

'*Why does it have to be rigid?*'

'*Why does it have to be usable?*'

'Perhaps the centre could be flexible so you could bend the pencil over your hand when using it.'

'Perhaps the centre could be a special shape. When you have used up the pencil on one side then you start again from the other end.'

These are only the beginnings of ideas. We can now apply the challenge process to the three thinking situations.

SITUATION A The car park problem.

Challenge Why treat the small size of the car park as a problem? Why not use it as an advantage? Only the best performers, judged by performance or by their peers, would have access to the car park. Use of the car park is now an incentive to be earned.

SITUATION B The new restaurant.

Challenge Why think only of selling cooked food? Think of selling special delicatessen-type food. Think of selling the tableware (plates, glasses, etc.).

SITUATION C The graffiti problem.

Challenge Why seek to remove all the graffiti? Just remove the ugly ones and leave the attractive ones. This should raise the standard and also get free decoration for the wall.

PROVOCATION

We come now to the principle of *provocation*. This is a fundamental principle in lateral thinking and in creativity.

The brain as a self-organizing system sets up patterns or sequences or tracks along which our thinking normally flows. This is the excellence of the brain and without such routine tracks life would be impossible as we should have to work out afresh every little thing. But these tracks have side tracks which we cannot get to from the main track. It is a sort of one-way system. If 'somehow' we can move 'laterally' to one of the side tracks then we can easily find our way back to the starting-point.

That is the essence of creativity. That is why all valued creative ideas are logical after you have seen them. That is also the basis for humour. In humour we are taken to the side track and immediately see the 'way back' or the logic of the humour.

It is this moving 'laterally' across patterns that gave rise to the term 'lateral thinking'. Instead of working harder in the same direction we move laterally to new concepts and new perceptions.

But how do we make these lateral moves? Challenge and the intention to change help but are not enough. That is why we need 'provocation'. Provocation provides a sort of stepping-stone so that we can step out of the usual track. Once out of the usual track we look around for other tracks.

In normal life you should only say something if there is a reason for saying it. The reasons come first and the conclusion next.

With a 'provocation' there is no reason for saying something until after it has been said. The provocaton provokes useful ideas, which then justify the provocation:

'*Po cars have square wheels*.'

This is a provocation. It is totally unreasonable in terms of our usual knowledge of wheels and cars. Yet from this provocation we move forward to the idea of 'intelligent suspension' where the suspension reacts in anticipation of the need so the axles follow the profile of the ground and the car rides smoothly even over rough ground.

The word 'po' was invented by me many years ago to 'signal' that a provocation was being used. You can think of it as standing for Provocative Operation. 'Po' says: 'What follows is a provocation.'

There is a problem of river pollution. The river gets ever more polluted as the pollution from different factories accumulates. So we put in a provocation:

'*Po each factory must be downstream of itself*.'

This sounds impossible. How can a factory be downstream of itself? But from this apparently illogical provocation comes a simple suggestion. Legislate so that a factory input must be just downstream of its own output. Now that factory has to be concerned about its output because that is part of its own input. I am told that this suggestion has now become law in some countries.

Our normal thinking demands that we be reasonable at every

step. Creative thinking does not. We use deliberate provocations which are not at all reasonable.

Movement

Provocations would be useless without the process of *movement*. This process was discussed along with the basic processes towards the beginning of the book. 'Movement' means moving forward from an idea or statement.

It is most important to realize that 'movement' is quite distinct from 'judgement'. Judgement is all about comparing something new with our past experience and experience boxes: is this correct or is it not? Movement is not at all interested in whether or not something is true, valid or correct. Movement is only interested in 'moving forward' from the provocation to something useful.

I must also emphasize, for those who have some experience of brainstorming, that movement is an 'active' mental operation. Delaying judgement, deferring judgement, withholding judgement, are all far too weak. Movement is an active mental process. We can develop the skill of movement.

Sometimes the 'intention' of moving forward from a provocation is enough. But there are also some formal methods of movement which we can try.

1. Extract a principle, concept or feature from the provocation. Take this and ignore the rest. Build an idea around this principle.
2. Focus on the difference between the provocation and what is normally done. Build an idea from some aspect of this difference.

3. Imagine, visualize (project) the provocation being put into action. Watch what happens 'moment to moment'. From this observation develop some ideas.

4. Pick out the positive aspects of the provocation and seek to work these into a new idea.

5. Seek some special circumstances under which the provocation would have a direct value.

As you build up your skill in 'movement' you will find yourself using these different processes and find that you are able to get movement from almost any provocation.

All these processes and the whole area of creative thinking are covered in much greater detail in my book *Serious Creativity*.*

Setting Up Provocations

Movement is what we do with provocations. But how do we set up provocations in the first place?

There may be ideas or suggestions that arise in the course of a discussion or that you have read about. Your natural tendency would be to judge these and to dismiss them if they seemed unreasonable. You now have an additional choice. You can still regard the suggestion as unreasonable but you can now choose to use it as a 'provocation'. So you set it up as a provocation (by placing 'po' before it) and then proceed to use movement to move towards a new idea.

So any arising idea can be treated by you as a provocation if

**Serious Creativity*, HarperCollins, 1993.

you so wish. It does not matter whether the person offering the idea knows anything about provocation – it is your choice.

There are also some systematic ways of setting up provocations.

1. *Escape.* We spell out something that we take for granted in the situation (this can never be negative). Then we cancel, negate, drop or remove what we have taken for granted. For example, we 'take for granted' that taxi drivers know the way. So our provocation is: 'Po taxi drivers do not know the way.' From this we move forward to the idea of 'learner taxis' which are marked in some way. These taxis would only be used by those who knew their way around the city and could instruct the driver. It would mean that learner drivers earned some income while they were learning.

2. *Reversal.* Here we take the 'normal direction' in which something is happening and reverse it or turn it in the opposite direction. The provocation 'Po cars have square wheels' is an example of this. We normally try to make wheels as round as possible. Here we go in the opposite direction and make them square.

3. *Exaggeration.* We take some dimension or measurement and exaggerate upwards or downwards beyond the normal range. The provocation 'Po police have six eyes' led to the idea of citizens' watch in 1971.

4. *Distortion.* We lay out the normal sequence or pattern of relationships and then deliberately alter, change or distort this. The provocation 'Po you close your letter after you

have posted it' seems impossible but leads to an interesting idea. You do not close your letter or put a stamp on it. A mail order house inserts a brochure or leaflet in your letter and then pays for the stamp and closes the letter. This is done by arrangement with the post office.

5. *Wishful thinking.* We say to ourselves: 'Po wouldn't it be nice if . . .' This should be a fantasy rather than a simple desire. We should not expect it to happen. It is not something we can work towards. The provocation 'Po the factory should be downstream of itself' is of this type.

The setting up of provocations should be deliberate and mechanical. You should never reject a provocation because it seems too bizarre and too impossible. You should not choose provocations that are along the way to some solution you have in mind – you will not get any provocation from these.

Learning lateral thinking is like learning to ride a bicycle. At first it seems awkward and contrary to your natural behaviour. How can anyone learn to ride a bicycle? As you practise and pick up skill it becomes easier and easier. Eventually you wonder why it ever seemed awkward. But you do have to work at it. There are also formal training courses given by certified trainers.*

We can now see how these provocative processes can be applied to the three thinking situations.

*For information on training in lateral thinking, please fax 0171–602 1779.

SITUATION A The car park problem.

Provocation 'Po (wouldn't it be nice if) each car carried its own car park with it.' We move forward from this to the idea of permanent vouchers for nearby car parks. We could even more forward to a more extreme idea of cars being built with hooks on the roof so they could be lifted into the air at appropriate places – so parking in the air.

SITUATION B The new restaurant.

Provocation We take for granted that restaurants serve food. So the escape-type provocation would be: 'Po a restaurant with no food.' From this we move forward to the idea of an elegant 'indoor picnic place'. Guests would bring their own hampers. Tableware, washing up and even drinks could be provided. There would also be a service charge.

SITUATION C The graffiti problem.

Provocation 'Po the graffiti were written very small' (exaggeration-type provocation). This would lead to the idea of projecting them on to the wall. This leads to the idea of projecting something on to the wall to hide the graffiti. For example, different coloured lights could neutralize the colour of the graffiti. If the graffiti were no longer readable there might be less motivation to put them on the wall.

RANDOM-ENTRY PROVOCATION

This is another form of provocation. It is also the simplest of all lateral thinking techniques.

The random-entry method is especially suitable for 'blank-sheet' creativity. You are asked to come up with creative ideas but do not know where to start. The method is also useful when you feel that you have exhausted all possible ideas and keep going back over the same ones again. When your thinking is stagnant the random-entry method can also help to get it going again.

The history of science is full of examples of how an apparently random event triggered an important idea. There is the famous story (probably untrue) of how Newton's thoughts on gravity were triggered by an apple which fell on his head as he was sitting reading in an orchard in Woolsthorp, Lincolnshire. There are many other stories of how a random event triggered an idea in a mind that had been thinking about the matter. The explanation is surprisingly simple.

The random event allows the mind of the thinker to start at a different point. Starting at a different point allows the mind to come towards the subject using a different track. This track then becomes usable as a fresh idea. In the asymmetric patterns formed in the brain, starting at a different point can give very different ideas because the mind is no longer constrained to follow traditional thinking.

In practice, how do we get this new starting-point?

That is where 'random entry' comes in. The simplest form of new starting-point is a 'random word'. (It is easiest to use nouns.) The random entry could also be an object, a picture or any other matter.

The main point is that the random word cannot in any sense be chosen. If it were to be chosen then the frame of choice would reflect our usual thinking.

A simple practical way is to have a list of sixty nouns and then to glance at your watch. Take the position of the 'seconds' hand. If this indicates 24 seconds then take word 24 on the list. In this way the word is not selected for any relevance to the subject.

At this point logicians get very, very anxious. They point out that if the 'word' has no relationship with the subject then any word would do for any subject and how can anything useful result?

This is why it is necessary to understand, at least in broad terms, how the brain works in order to devise deliberate thinking tools. The random word which is an extremely simple and powerful tool arises directly from an understanding of patterning systems.

A person living in a smallish town always takes the same road on leaving his house. This road can get him to wherever he wants to go. One day his car breaks down on the outskirts of the town. He has to walk home. He wants the most direct route. He asks directions. He finds himself reaching his house by a road he would never have thought of taking on leaving his house. There is no magic. At the centre there is one dominant road which he always takes. At the periphery there are many possible roads all of which can lead back to the house. So if you start at the periphery you increase the chance of opening up new tracks. That is the logical explanation of why the random-entry method works.

In practice the method is extremely easy to use. You have the subject or thinking need, you obtain a random word and you connect them with a 'po' to indicate provocation.

'Copier po nose' leads to the idea of using 'smell' as an indicator. If the copier is running short of paper or toner then it emits a special signal smell. Anyone in the vicinity then hurries to replenish supplies. Smell has the advantage that you do not have to be looking at an indicator on the machine.

You should never try several random words just because you do not like the first one. Nor should you move to another word. Nor should you first list the attributes of the word. Nor should you hop from one association to another. In all these cases you would not be using the 'provocative' nature of the random word but just seeking for an 'easy fit'.

We can now see how this random-entry method might work with the three thinking situations.

SITUATION A Car park problem.

Random Provocation The random word is 'sequin'. Obviously this word could never have been selected as relevant to the car park problem. Sequins work because there are many of them. So divide the car park up into sections and assign a section to each department. Let them decide how to use their section.

SITUATION B The new restaurant.

Random Provocation The random word is 'shadow'. This

directly suggests Indonesia shadow puppets. A shadow puppet show would be most suitable for a restaurant because it takes up so little space. The idea can also be expanded to a theatre restaurant so that the play is advertised as well as the restaurant. A shadow is also something which 'follows' the real thing. So guests who have dined at the restaurant can be sent periodic reminders in the form of new menus or new dishes. They can also be sent vouchers which could be used directly or given to others as presents.

SITUATION C The graffiti problem.

Random Provocation The random word is 'bikini'. This immediately suggests that if there is something attractive on the wall then people are less likely to deface it. Another suggestion is to turn the wall into a poster site. The organization selling the poster sites then has the responsibility of monitoring the wall and keeping it clean. This might apply even if only part of the wall was so used.

We come now to the end of the Creative Approach in the **PO** stage of thinking. As always, the outputs of the **PO** stage are ideas and possibilities. These link up the starting position as determined by the **LO** stage and with the thinking purpose as determined in the **TO** stage.

We continue on with the fourth and final approach used in the **PO** stage. This is the approach of 'design and assembly'.

4. The Design and Assembly Approach

This is the fourth and last of the approaches used in the **PO** stage of thinking.

The design and assembly approach puts things together to achieve the purpose of the thinking. This is different from the *search for a routine approach* because in that approach the action is already laid out and pre-set. In the *general approach* we narrow down from a broadly stated need to specific ways of carrying out that need. In the *creative approach* we generate ideas and then modify them to see if they will suit our purpose.

The design and assembly approach is constructive. We put things together. This assembly is creative in the sense that what is produced may be something new. But the components, ingredients or elements that have been assembled need not be new in themselves. The standard words of the alphabet can be assembled to give many words. Some of the elements used in the approach may indeed be new in themselves or the overall concept may be new.

An architect has a 'design brief'. The architect is asked to design a house for a certain site. This house should have three bedrooms, a large room for working at home, a kitchen with a view, a garage for two cars, a large room for entertaining and plenty of storage space. The architect could look through a book of standard designs and select the nearest. This would be the 'search for a routine' approach. More usually, the architect will put together a design from known components to achieve the design brief. In this case of the architect the design may be no more than an assembly of components which are then made to fit in with one another.

A dress designer has a general 'look' that he or she wants to achieve. The designer then tries out different approaches to achieving this look. Some of the approaches might be borrowed from traditional costumes, some may come from the designer's past, some might be new tries. There is a certain amount of trial and error. A good designer is able to 'project' and to imagine what something will look like instead of having to make up every idea.

LIST THE NEEDS

One approach to design is to list the needs. This gives a sort of mould for the final outcome. The designer then works to fill this mould.

Each need may be satisfied separately. These separate elements are then brought together and an attempt is made to fashion them into a coherent whole. This process is similar to that of the architect described above. If we were designing a mobile chair for an invalid the 'needs list' might include:

- quiet
- non-polluting
- easy to refuel
- easy to control
- easy to get on and off
- powerful
- small in size.

Many of the above requirements would lead immediately to

consideration of an electric motor. This is quiet, non-polluting, powerful, easy to control, easy to refuel, small in size, etc. So far, the process is similar to a 'search for routine'. Then the chair part has to be built around the motor. This is where the design comes in. The constraints and important factors such as 'safety' are also brought in as considerations (the CAF operation in the CoRT lessons).

If you were designing ballot papers for an election there might be the following list of needs:

- easy to understand
- minimum wordage
- visual communication
- clear indication as to whom is being selected
- confirmation that the selection is an intended response in standard places
- easy to read (possibly readable by machine)
- difficult to spoil unless this is intended
- difficult to forge.

The designer would then attempt to incorporate all these requirements in the design. There might come a point when a new idea was needed. This would then become a focus for 'creative thinking'. For example: how do we visually indicate a candidate for those who have poor eyesight or cannot read?

LEAD WITH PRIORITIES

Here we choose one or two priorities and design around these. For example, we might decide that the avoidance of confusion was the top priority in the ballot paper. So we set out to design a ballot paper which was clear and explicit. Having established this then we seek to add on the other needs or to modify the initial design to accommodate the other needs and the constraints.

The choice of the lead priorities is up to the designer. It may be that these are indeed the top priorities in the design brief. Or it may be that these needs are going to be the most difficult to satisfy, so we might as well give all our attention to these and then look at the easier needs later. So a designer of a new fast food would look at the cost factor first. If the proposed food is too expensive then the design becomes useless. Taste and convenience can be added later. The designer of 'health foods' would, however, first attend to the 'health' aspect. How could it be genuinely claimed that there was a health aspect?

In designing a holiday the lead priority might be the weather. Or it might be both weather and cost. Another priority might be to satisfy the champion grumbler, who would otherwise ruin the holiday.

CONCEPT FIRST

Sometimes the designer may think of an overall concept first and then look to see how the different needs can be hitched on to that. In the case of a theme park the overall concept is obvious. In the case of a bookcase the overall concept might be 'monastic seriousness' or 'lightness' or 'source of colour'. In each case the design would have to be strong enough and large enough to carry the books and would have to fit the specified dimensions.

Concepts may be original or may be borrowed from other sources. In clothes design there may be an overall 'season look', which different designers interpret in different ways. There are similar fashions with motor cars.

In designing a meal there may also be an overall concept such as 'Mediterranean' or 'adventurous' or 'traditional' or 'nouvelle cuisine' or 'nursery', etc.

Designers may work towards a 'general' end determined by the concept and then seek to shape the result to satisfy the needs of the design brief. Famous architects usually work this way. Their work is distinctive with their own style. Yet all the required elements are included in the final design.

PARALLEL INPUT

Negotiations, in theory, should be designed outputs rather than battles for supremacy. The final design should accommodate the values, needs and fears of the different parties. Their perceptions have to be taken into account.

In order to achieve this sort of design it is first necessary to lay everything down in parallel. It is useless to argue at every point whether one set of values is superior to another set of values and whether one perception is more correct than another.

The reason why the *Six Thinking Hats* framework has been so eagerly taken up by business is that it provides a simple framework for constructive design. How do we design a way forward? This is quite different from trying to reach an output through arguing who is right and who is wrong.

Under the white hat all information is put down in parallel even when the information may be contradictory.

Under the yellow hat the perceived benefits and values are laid down in parallel.

Under the black hat the fears, dangers and potential problems are laid down in parallel.

Under the red hat there is an opportunity to express feelings, intuition and emotions.

Under the green hat there is the attempt to design all this into an outcome that would be acceptable to both sides.

This outcome may now be subjected to yellow, black and red hats all over again.

EVERYDAY DESIGN

There is nothing magic about design. We do it every day. Whenever you write something you are putting together standard words to achieve the expression or communication of what you want to communicate.

When you get dressed in the morning you are putting together available clothes to serve some purpose: comfort, fashion, keeping warm, etc.

Whenever you cook a meal you are designing a meal, unless you are following a routine which determines what you have every day.

Anything which is not routine is design. Design may assemble different routines, just as designing a journey across town may involve putting together different standard bus routes to get you to where you want to go. In this particular example, analysis and design work from opposite ends. Analysis would seek to break down the overall journey into standard segments. Design would seek to build up the journey by assembling standard segments. Where the desired outcome is as specific as a determined destination then design and analysis can be used interchangeably. But where the outcome is more open-ended then it might not be possible to analyse what is not yet there. Devising new headgear for a police officer might involve analysing the needs and requirements but then it requires design. You cannot analyse the final outcome because the only outcome you have at the beginning is the existing headgear. You might seek to remedy defects in this but that is problem solving not design. There are new ideas which might be included which do not relate to existing problems. For example, the new headgear might become a usable weapon.

We can now try the *design and assembly* approach on the three thinking situations.

SITUATION A The car park problem.

Design Approach The design brief might be: a solution that satisfies all those who want to use the car park – matching needs with availability of space. If there were fewer cars and more people per car those needs could be satisfied. So the suggestion is to give car park access only to those who bring in two other (or more) fellow workers with them.

SITUATION B The new restaurant.

Design Approach The list of needs might include:

- publicity
- reputation

- being noticed
- satisfied customers
- fashion.

The result might be employing a publicist who would be paid a fee plus a commission on all business in the first six months.

SITUATION C The graffiti problem.

Design Approach We need to discourage graffiti artists without the cost of continual surveillance or the cost of repeated cleaning. Perhaps a bad smell (like hydrogen sulphide) near the wall might discourage graffiti artists.

Summary of the PO Stage

The **PO** stage of thinking is the generative and productive stage of thinking. It is this stage which links up where we are now with where we want to be.

The **PO** stage generates possibilities. Some are better than others. Some need to be developed further before they are evaluated. Some of the possibilities do not fit all the constraints and requirements. Some will be more practical than others. Some will be more expensive than others.

The important point to remember is that it is the function of the **PO** stage to generate 'possibilities'. If you immediately evaluate each possibility as it arises then you are going to stay firmly within your own thinking. There has to be evaluation before an idea is to be used. This evaluation takes place in the next or **SO** stage of thinking. Generate as many possibilities as you can, develop them and then evaluate them, and choose the best for action. Never feel that you can simplify the choice stage by reducing the number of possible alternatives. That is bad thinking and dangerous thinking. It is not possible to choose the best outcome as you go along. The generative stage does have to be separated from the evaluation stage. It is only if you use the 'search for routine' approach that you do need to be right at every stage. Otherwise you will end up using the wrong box. But that is only one of the four approaches.

The four approaches put forward in this section on the **PO** stage of thinking do overlap but they also exist clearly in their own right.

1. The *search for a routine approach* means looking back into our experience to find out what to do. The link between the situation and the action routine is 'identifying' the *box* into which the situation fits. We can use analysis to break down complex situations to make the identification easier.

2. In the *general approach* we define the needs in very broad and general terms. Then we seek to make these more and more specific until in the end we have a practical way of achieving what we want.

3. In the *creative approach* we set out to generate ideas. We then examine these to see if they meet our needs. We seek to modify the ideas to serve our purpose.

4. In the *design and assembly approach* we put together different elements to build up what we want.

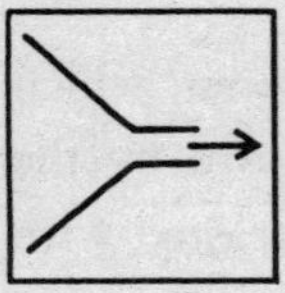

SO

What is the Outcome?

So . . .
So what?
So what is the outcome?
So what do we do?
So this is what we do?

The purpose of the **SO** stage of thinking is to take the possibilities produced by the **PO** stage and to produce an outcome from them. At the end of the **PO** stage the possibilities are merely possibilities. We have to develop them and evaluate them before they can be regarded as usable ideas. Then we have to choose between the many usable ideas to end up with the one which we decide to use. So the overall purpose of the **SO** stage is development and choice. At the end of the **SO** stage we should have the chosen idea, which we then take forward to the **GO** stage for action.

This overall process may sometimes be shortened. For example, if the purpose of thinking was to obtain some information and this information was easily obtained, the thinker might go directly from the **LO** stage to the **GO** stage. In the same way, if the *search for a routine* approach in the **PO** stage found just such a routine, the thinker might proceed directly to the **GO** stage. Even in this case, however, the evaluation part of the **SO** stage would be advisable. In general it is best to stick to the full framework but some of the stages may, at times, be quite short.

The symbol for the **SO** stage shows a *reducing process*, which then produces one outcome. This outcome is shown by the single arrow moving forwards. This may be contrasted with the symbol for the **PO** stage which produced many 'possibilities'.

Sequence

The sequence within the **SO** stage is as follows:

DEVELOPMENT
to
EVALUATION
to
CHOICE
to
DECISION
to
ACTION (in the **GO** stage)

Development of Possibilities

Some of the possibilities produced by the generative processes of the **PO** stage may be no more than initial ideas or the beginnings of ideas. They are indeed possibilities but they need working on before they can be evaluated. This is particularly true with the output from the 'creative approach' in the **PO** stage. Even the output from a 'search for routine' approach may need to be modified or adapted to circumstances.

You should not jump immediately into the evaluation and choice aspects of the **SO** stage. Spend some time improving and building up the ideas.

SHAPING IDEAS

Imagine a potter 'shaping' a pot on the spinning wheel. Pressure is applied at the right place to obtain the shape which the potter desires.

In the creative process we do not design ideas to fit the constraints but generate the ideas and then bring in the constraints to shape the idea.

Some of the *shaping* constraints may be very general. For example, an idea must be made legal. Can we shape this idea so that it is indeed legal? The idea of monopoly car parks restricted to one make of car may not be legal but subsidization by manufacturers to reduce the cost for their make of car might be legal. Ideas must be shaped to fit fire and building regulations. The idea may be too bulky or too complex and so has to be shaped to be smaller or simpler.

There are also very particular constraints which may have to be brought into the shaping process. The idea may have to be approved by one particular person, who is known to have certain dislikes. How can the idea be shaped to avoid these dislikes?

TAILORING

A tailor cuts the suit to fit the cloth that is available. So tailoring is altering an idea to *fit* the particular resources of the person or organization that is going to act on the idea.

The idea may be wonderful in itself and may have been successfully shaped by all the constraints. But is the idea suitable for us?

An idea that might be suitable for a large organization with its own sales team might be quite unsuitable for a small organization without a sales team. An idea that might be suitable for an extrovert and bold person might be quite unsuitable for an introverted and shy person. The idea is excellent but the fit is not.

We ask: what sort of organization or person could act on this idea? Then we ask: is that our sort of organization or person? If the answer is that it is not our sort of organization or person then we seek to 'tailor' the idea to fit our resources. A small restaurant could not afford to have free meal vouchers given away in a supermarket because the restaurant would be swamped. But vouchers limited to a specific date and time might be possible.

STRENGTHEN THE IDEA

We note the strength, power or value of the suggested possibility. Then we try to strengthen it even further. The first expression of an idea may not exploit the full potential of the idea. For instance, a lottery could be made even more powerful if participants were allowed to go for either the 'jackpot' prize or a large number of smaller prizes. In practice they would probably go for both and buy two tickets instead of just one. So do not be satisfied just because an idea seems good. It may be possible to make it even better.

FAULT CORRECTION

This is an obvious part of the development of any idea. There can be weaknesses, faults and defects. We seek to put these right. If the problems are serious then this can become a whole thinking exercise in itself. Perhaps the promotional idea can backfire – how do we remove that risk? Perhaps the weakness in the idea is that it all depends on one person. Can that be remedied? Perhaps the major defect of the idea is that it is going to take too long. Can it be done in a shorter time?

Here the Black Thinking Hat is used to list all the defects and potential dangers. This is not as part of an evaluation process but as part of the development process. You seek to overcome the defects.

PRACTICALITY

This is obviously extremely important. Practicality can come under any of the previous development headings but it also needs 'attention directing' in its own right.

How practical is this idea? Can the idea be made more practical?

Practicality is usually less exciting than novelty or benefits, so creative people sometimes tend to ignore practicality. The development process must then work to make the idea practical.

A practical idea is one which could be used immediately in the existing state of affairs without waiting for major changes.

ACCEPTANCE

An idea may be wonderful in itself but not 'acceptable'. The idea may not be acceptable at a particular point in time or to a particular group. If an idea for increasing productivity is not acceptable to the workforce or to the unions then the idea is dead. If an investment idea is not acceptable to the board then that idea is dead.

Projecting whether an idea will be acceptable or not is a matter of looking into the perceptions of others. The suggestion that limited space in a car park be used as a reward for the hardest workers might not be acceptable to those who live off the public transport system and have to use their cars to get to work.

So we work to make an idea acceptable. Sometimes this may only be a matter of presentation of the idea. Sometimes it may be a matter of a minor addition. Sometimes the whole idea needs changing. The car park idea might be made acceptable by making exceptions for those who really had to use their cars.

COST

How expensive is the idea going to be? How expensive to set up? How expensive to run?

Attention to cost is fundamental and will have been included in the shaping and tailoring processes. There is usually a budget and ideas have to be tailored to this. A high cost would also have surfaced under attention to defects. But cost is so important that it also needs direct attention in its own right.

- What is the cost in money terms?
- What is the cost in management time?
- What is the cost in disruption and hassle?

All these matters will emerge again under the evaluation of an idea. At this point we look at these matters in order to improve the idea. Could we carry out the idea in partnership with someone else and so reduce the cost? Could we have the object made in China at a lower price? Could we try it out in a smaller area?

SIMPLER

When first conceived, ideas are always much more complex than they need to be. This is particularly true of creative ideas. So the development effort is directed at simplifying the idea. Very often an idea can be simplified without losing any of its value.

The idea of enlarging the goalposts in a soccer match when there is no score can be made simpler by removing the goalkeeper for a short period until there is a score.

TAKE THE CONCEPT

Sometimes we can take the 'concept' out of a possibility and then apply this concept in a totally different way. This is also part of the development process.

What is the concept here? How can we apply that concept in a better way?

The concept of providing customers with video catalogues could be changed to down-loading catalogues from broadcast

TV in the early hours of the morning. Or customers might bring their own tapes and have catalogues copied on to them according to their own needs. So there would be customized catalogues organized through a CD-ROM computer. Another extension of the basic concept would be for customers to request details and price lists over the phone and for these to be delivered by fax.

Evaluation and Assessment

Having done our best to develop the possibilities into powerful ideas we must at some stage move towards evaluation and assessment.

- Is this idea worth doing?
- Can it be done?

There are always these two aspects. If the idea is not worth doing then we need not bother about how to do it. If the idea is worth doing then we have to assess whether it can be done or whether we can do it.

In the Six Thinking Hats framework the following hats would be used for evaluation.

The yellow hat to search for values and benefits.

The black hat to search for dangers, problems and potential problems.

The white hat to see if the suggestion fits with what we know about the situation.

In the CoRT Thinking Programme the following simple tools are used:

PMI to look for the Plus, Minus and Interesting points about the idea.

C&S to follow the idea forward to see what would happen – to assess the consequences.

VALUES AND BENEFITS

It is possible to make a distinction between *values* and *benefits*. We could say that the value resides in the thing itself and the benefit is the value a person gets from that thing. In other words, benefits are always people-related.

The benefits of owning a bar of gold could be as follows:

- hedge against inflation
- something to boast about
- can be sold for the money
- useful as a heavy doorstop
- can be turned into jewellery
- collateral for a loan.

These benefits will depend on the person and the circumstances. For example, when interest rates are high you get no interest on the money locked up in the gold bar. You would be better off having the money and investing it. In times of inflation, on the other hand, gold might hold its value more than money. Showing off might be a benefit to some people but to others it would be a danger because it might attract burglars.

In general there is not much to be gained by making this

distinction between benefits and value. Value is a sort of deposit of potential benefits. The two can, however, be used more or less interchangeably.

It is always worth assessing the values and benefits first. If the values and benefits are low or absent then clearly there is no need to go further, because the idea is not worth using. When you are making your best effort to find value and still cannot find it then the idea can be dropped – or put into storage.

If, however, you do find considerable values and benefits then you are more motivated to overcome the difficulties that there may be in the suggestion. You will also be more motivated to find ways of carrying out the suggestion.

The search for values and benefits is not easy. You really have to make an effort.

- What are the benefits?
- For whom are the benefits?
- How do they arise?
- On what do the benefits depend?
- How large are the benefits?
- How secure are the benefits?

There is a suggestion of making a special cap for toothpaste tubes. This special cap would have a large hole through it from side to side. What are the benefits?

'*The user could hang the toothpaste tubes on hooks. Different members of the family might have different brands.*'

'*The retailer could hang the toothpaste on racks and so save valuable shelf space.*'

'*The manufacturer might not have to put the toothpaste into cardboard boxes. The reduction in the use of cardboard would help with waste disposal and also require fewer trees to be felled, etc.*'

When looking for values and benefits we do need to look into the future. How long will the benefits last? Are there possible circumstances under which the benefits would disappear? Will further benefits appear later?

In assessing difficulties we do have to look hard into the future for potential trouble. With benefits, however, future benefits are usually not much use unless there are also immediate benefits. This is not totally true, otherwise it would be impossible to sell life insurance. Investment decisions are also made on a longer-term basis. But, in general, ideas are not seen as attractive unless there are immediate benefits.

Benefits may include:

- more of the same value
- new values
- variety
- less cost
- convenience
- less hassle/trouble
- simpler
- prestige
- 'feel-good' factor
- security
- comfort
- excitement
- peace.

It is important to be 'sensitive' to values and benefits. This means being ready to see values and benefits even if they are not obvious. Sometimes we only look for the very obvious values like saving money. Such values as 'peace of mind' are often ignored but in practice are very important.

So you list the perceived values and benefits for each of the possibilities.

DIFFICULTIES AND DANGERS

Obviously matters like *risk* and *difficulty in implementation* could be noted here, but they will be considered later. At this point we say, 'Suppose it were possible to implement the idea, what would be the difficulties and dangers?'

If the difficulties and dangers are considerable and cannot be overcome, then we do not even need to work out the feasibility of the idea because we do not want to use it.

'*The idea might upset some people.*'

'*The idea might damage our reputation or something else we are doing.*'

'*The idea might be too expensive or the costs might escalate.*'

'*The product might be harmful.*'

'*The idea may not work at all.*'

'*The idea is too complex.*'

'*The idea has little general appeal.*'

The three main aspects of this critical evaluation are:

1. That the idea fails to deliver what it is supposed to deliver.

2. That the idea actually causes damage or harm to us, to our reputation or to others.

3. That the cost is too high.

In this sort of evaluation we need to do a lot of 'projection' thinking. We need to look ahead to imagine and to visualize what might happen. We need to imagine different circumstances and combinations of circumstances. We may need to imagine the response of competitors. If we lower air fares and they lower them further we may suffer most.

The list of negative points should now be laid out.

If the idea is seen to be very beneficial then one final attempt might be made to overcome the difficulties discovered at this point. In theory such difficulties should have been attended to in the 'development' stage but they may not have been noticed.

FEASIBILITY

This is the third arm of evaluation. We like the idea. It has benefits. The difficulties are not serious. So we want to go ahead. Can we do it? Is the idea feasible – for us? At this point feasibility is always considered in terms of who is actually going to be using the idea.

'*Are there mechanisms for doing it?*'

'*Can the idea be put through the usual channels?*'

'*Do we have the resources (people, time, money) to do it?*'

'*Do we have the motivation to do it?*'

'*Do we have the energy to do it?*'

'*Will the idea get approval and acceptance?*'

'*How will it interfere with other things we are doing?*'

'*Do I really want to do it?*'

There are good ideas which we feel we ought to do but do not really want to do. There are other ideas which may not be so good but which we do want to do. Motivation is part of feasibility. If there is no motivation then things do not get done even when it is quite possible to do them. So at this point some red hat assessment of feelings can be in order.

There may be existing mechanisms through which the idea can be carried out. Or, we may have to set up new mechanisms. We may set out to seek partners.

How we set up something to carry out the idea may well become a whole new thinking focus in itself. The purpose (**TO** stage) of our thinking would be: how do we carry out this idea?

The **SO** stage of thinking need not work out the full details of implementation. That will be done in the **GO** stage. But the assessment of feasibility does need to end up with a clear idea of whether the idea is feasible or not:

1. Definitely feasible
2. Feasible with some effort and some adjustments
3. Feasible with difficulty
4. Not feasible at all.

Choice

Both development and evaluation look at each idea in isolation. How do we develop that idea? How do we evaluate that idea? At this point:

- We may have *no ideas* attractive enough for us to want to go forward.
- We may have *one idea* which is obviously much better than the others.
- We may have *several good ideas* and need to choose between them.
- We may have a *huge number* of apparently good ideas.

A beautiful lady with a number of ardent suitors can only marry one of them. So she has to make a choice.

Here we shall assume that we can only use one of the feasible ideas. This is not always true because there are many occasions when we can use several of the ideas. In any case, the ideas that are not chosen are not discarded but can be put into storage for future consideration or even 'sold' to another organization.

At this point in the thinking process we can be quite ruthless. We set up our priorities and our selection basis, and then we put aside those that do not make it.

For example, you might have a very simple selection basis:

'*I am only going to consider those ideas that I feel strongly about.*'

This is pure Red Hat selection.

STRONGER AND WEAKER

This is a very simple method of selection. You divide all the possibilities into two groups: the stronger group and the weaker group. This composite assessment of *stronger* and *weaker* is based on a general feeling of benefits, dangers, feasibility and intuition.

Then you divide the *stronger* group into stronger and weaker.

You continue until you only have a few possibilities left. You then compare these in a more detailed way.

IN AND OUT

You may choose some quality or characteristic which all usable ideas have to have. For example, in choosing a place to live you may say, 'It must be within one hour's travel time of where I work.' Possibilities which have this characteristic are included *in*. The others remain *out*.

You may choose some quality or characteristic which must not be part of any usable idea. For example you may say: 'I do not want any idea which is going to be expensive.' You therefore throw out all ideas which are expensive. Those which are not expensive remain 'in'.

There may be more than one 'in' characteristic and more than one 'out' characteristic.

PRIORITIES

Having evaluated the ideas, you will have become conscious of the types of benefits offered and also the difficulties. You may also return to the **TO** stage to redefine the needs of your thinking. With what do you want to end up? From this you should be able to put together a list of priorities as a basis for selection. There might be as many as twelve or as few as four.

You now check each of the possibilities against this list. These may be your original possibilities or those that remain after the selection procedures suggested above. You can give a 'yes' or 'no' depending on whether the possibility meets that particular priority. You now look to see which possibilities meet most of the priorities.

If you wish you can give a degree of importance to each priority. So a possibility that meets priority number one gets 10 points but a possibility that meets priority number ten only gets 1 point. Then add up the scores and the winner may be the possibility you ought to choose.

Another way is not to use a simple 'yes' or 'no' to indicate whether a possibility meets a priority, but to give a 'degree' of meeting ranging from 1 to 5. So a possibility that fully meets the priority gets a 5 but one that only just meets it gets a 1.

Both these methods can be combined – but it does get rather complicated. The purpose is to turn qualities into quantities and then allow the larger quantity to make our choice.

DIRECT COMPARISON

When the possibilities have been reduced to a few then it becomes possible to make direct comparisons between the possibilities.

'*What are the benefits of this possibility compared to that one?*'

'*What are the difficulties with this possibility compared to that one?*'

'How do they differ in feasibility?'

'Which of the benefits and dangers are more important to us?'

GREED, FEAR AND LAZINESS

In another book, *De Bono's Thinking Course*,* I suggest a simple way of making a choice. This is based on the three elements of greed, fear and laziness. So we take each possibility in turn and see which of these three apply.

'I like this idea because it offers great benefits' (greed element).

'I don't like this idea because of the uncertainties and dangers' (fear element).

'I don't like this idea because it is too complicated and involves too much effort' (laziness element).

Usually the elements will be combined, but in each case there will be a dominant element which inclines you to choose the idea or to reject it.

FINAL EVALUATION

Once you have made your choice then you should carry out a final evaluation.

- What indeed are the expected benefits?
- What are the possible problems?
- How feasible is it?

There is a need to look carefully at the consequences of putting the idea into action.

**De Bono's Thinking Course*, BBC Publications, 1983; new edition, 1993.

Decision

Decision is often used interchangeably with 'choice'. You might decide which alternative to choose. You might decide which road to take. The lady might decide which suitor to marry.

In this section I shall be treating 'decision' in the sense of go/no go. Do we do something or do we not? This is a very common use of decision. Do we move to another town or do we not? Do I take this job offer or do I not?

We can also apply the decision process to the outcome of the choice stage. We have selected the option we prefer from amongst the possibilities. Now do we go ahead with that option or do we not?

You could say that the decision has already been made in the choice stage but there are many considerations that fit more easily into the decision stage. Such considerations will be considered here.

DECISION FRAME

- What is the frame for the decision?
- Who is deciding?
- Is this a final decision or only one stage?
- Who is competent to make the decision?

This process looks at the background of the decision rather than at the contents. The decision made in a research department is not the same as an investment decision made at board level. Does a wife make a decision on her own or should the family come into it? Who is in the best position to decide what career you should follow?

DECISION NEED

- Why do we need to make this decision?
- What do we hope to get from this decision?
- What happens if we do nothing?
- What happens if we wait?
- Who needs this decision?
- Is the decision a luxury or a necessity?

This becomes a very difficult area because all change involves risk. There are therefore people who argue against any decision because of the risk. Yet there are times when not taking a decision is actually a bigger risk. It is usually difficult to see this. Opportunities may disappear. Things may get steadily worse without anyone noticing. Your competitors may move ahead. The danger of doing nothing will eventually become clear, but by then it may be too late to do anything about it. Famous organizations have gone out of business on this basis. They believed that maintenance was enough.

DECISION PRESSURE

- What is the pressure to make a decision?
- Is this a crisis?
- Is there a time pressure?
- Who is exerting the pressure?
- What is the hurry?

Certain things have time-limits. Applications might have to be in by a certain date. Prices change. Someone may need to make a decision.

SCENARIO

- What is the scenario in which we are making this decision?
- What is the future scenario going to look like?

We look not only at the consequences of the decision but also at the world in which the decision is going to be operating. We can only make a guess about the future. We can make a *best case guess* and a *worst case guess* and then seek to design our decision to be of value anywhere between these two extremes.

RISK

This is an extremely important element in decision, in choice, in evaluation, etc. Risk is considered here because at the decision stage an assessment of risk is essential. There are many different types of risk.

- The idea may not work out as we believe it should.
- The idea may be badly carried out.
- The idea may fail to reach its objective or target.
- The idea may do us damage.
- Circumstances might change and make the idea useless or dangerous.
- Competitive response might undo the idea or cause us damage.
- Things might change (interest rates, regulations, etc.).

So there are *shortfall* risks, where the idea does not work out as well as hoped.

Then there are *danger* risks, where we end up worse off than when we started.

There are also *uncertainty* risks, where unforeseen changes may lead to either of the above.

We need to be aware of risk. We also need to seek to reduce risk.

We can reduce operating risk by careful planning and proper training.

We can seek to test the idea in a pilot scheme, a test market or with focus groups.

We can seek to limit damage by designing a *fall-back position* or a *way-out position*.

We can seek to reduce risk by insurance, by hedging or by using financial derivatives.

We need not put all our eggs into one basket.

Anything involving the future involves risk. Even carrying on the same routines involves risk in a changing world. Blacksmiths are largely out of business through no fault of their own.

OUTCOME

So having considered the frame for the decision, the need and the pressures, and having considered the risk and the benefits of the chosen option, we have to make the decision. The decision is always a balance between needs, benefits and risk. If the need is such that doing nothing is an equal risk then the risk cancels out. We seek to be cautious and we seek to reduce risk as much as possible through design and back-up. If the need is great the benefits become powerful. So in the end it is need that drives decision.

We do need to do something. This is the best thing we can do.

Looking Back: the Reasons

When a choice or decision has been made it is very useful to look back and to spell out in detail the reasons why the choice or decision was made. Why was this chosen? Why was this other option rejected? Why was the decision made?

'*I made this decision because I believe that things will get worse if we do nothing. These are the reasons why I believe this . . .*'

'*I made this choice because the benefits offered are as follows . . . All of these are important and feasible.*'

'*I rejected that option because it requires skills we do not have.*'

'*I rejected that option because it just does not fit our style.*'

'*I made this decision because it feels right – the basis was intuition.*'

When you do this you will often be surprised by how weak and feeble the reasons now seem. Did you really choose or decide on that basis? Would you really justify your decision in this way?

This *hindsight check* is very useful. It can sometimes go back and force us to reconsider a choice or a decision. This check can also reveal that in the end the decision was intuitive, or Red Hat. This does not mean that it was wrong. But we should know about it.

There can also be a final Red Hat:

- What do I feel about this decision?
- Am I happy with this decision?

Summary of the **SO** Stage

The purpose of the **SO** stage is to take the possibilities delivered by the generative **PO** stage and to reduce these to a single choice – to something that can be acted on.

There is the *development* stage in which ideas are developed further. They are built up. They are strengthened. The defects are overcome. The ideas are made more practical, more acceptable and simpler. This is a creative and constructive stage in which we seek to make the best of an idea.

Then comes the *evaluation* stage. Each idea is now evaluated. What are the benefits and values? What are the difficulties and dangers? Is the idea feasible for us? At this stage we are still dealing with each possibility separately.

Next comes the *choice* stage, in which one idea must be selected from the number of available ideas (it does not always have to be one). There are various ways of carrying out this choice. Some simple methods can reduce the number of possibilities to a point where direct comparisons can be made.

Finally there is the *decision* stage. Do we proceed with the suggested idea or action or do we not proceed? We need to examine the need for the decision, the pressures and the framing. We need to assess the risk and seek ways of reducing this. If the need and expected rewards exceed the risk then we decide to go ahead.

At this point a chosen, usable idea is delivered to the final stage of thinking: the **GO** stage.

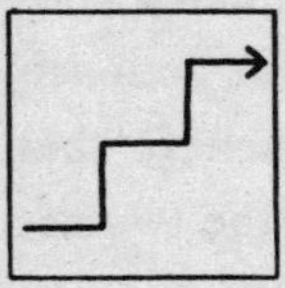

GO

Putting the Thinking to Work

Go!
Go forward
Go ahead
Let's **go**
Go to it
Get **go**ing

The symbol indicates moving forwards and upwards step by step. It suggests building something upwards. It suggests being constructive. The line is a solid line. It is no longer a possibility. We are making it happen.

It is perfectly true that *action* is not a necessary part of all thinking. The purpose of the thinking might have been to collect specific information. The purpose of the thinking might have been general exploration. The purpose of the thinking might have been understanding something through analysis. The purpose of the thinking might have been to solve a mental problem as in mathematics. The purpose of the thinking might have been to write something. The purpose of the thinking might have been to design some action which is then passed on to someone else to implement. There are many other instances in which action is not required at the end of thinking. Even so the **GO** stage rounds off the thinking. If the purpose of thinking is to produce a report then you produce that report.

It is a bad mistake, however, to believe that all thinking ends without action. It is a bad mistake to believe that action is someone else's business. It is a bad mistake to believe that there are 'thinkers' and there are 'doers' and that the two are separate. This is a false idea encouraged by the academic tradition. 'Doing' is supposed to be for people who cannot think. 'Doing' is supposed to be easy.

This mistaken view was encouraged by Socrates in particular and the Gang of Three in general. Socrates believed that 'knowledge was all'. If you only had the right knowledge then you would do the right actions. That part did not need thinking about. There is some truth in this. If you are an experienced car driver then it is enough to know the route to your destination. The driving part is easy and routine. There was a time when the world was rather like this: simple routine actions performed in an unchanging world. Today things are different. The world is changing. Action is no longer simple and obvious.

Operacy

Many years ago I invented the word 'operacy'. There was a reason for this. Education prided itself on being concerned with 'numeracy' (which was all about numbers and mathematics) and 'literacy' (which was all about the written word). Yet when youngsters left school they moved out into a world in which action was required. It was no longer a matter of reacting to something which was put in front of you. It was no longer a matter of being given all the information and asked to solve a problem. You had to take initiatives. You had to find the information. You had to generate alternatives, make decisions and take action. It seemed to me that 'operacy' was also important. Numeracy and literacy were not enough.

Operacy covers the broad skills of action, of making things happen.

Simple Output

The purpose of the **GO** stage of thinking is to link the output of the **SO** stage back to the **TO** stage. Obviously, it is possible to divide thinking into two separate parts.

- *Part 1:* 'I want to end up with a solution to this problem.'
- *Part 2:* 'I want to end up with a way of putting the solution to work.'

In some cases there is no choice because the implementation of the outcome of the thinking is as complex as the thinking itself. In less complex matters, however, the **GO** stage indicates the action needed to achieve the overall result – for example solving the problem. The importance of including this action under the **GO** stage is that the problem solution has to be practical because you are going to consider how to apply it. You are not just going to leave it in the air as a 'solution' for someone else to use.

By 'simple output' I mean those situations where almost all the thinking work has been done before the **GO** stage is reached. A list of such situations was given above. In such cases the **GO** stage may be no more than a summary.

'I have explored the subject and obtained as much information as possible.'

'I have explored the subject and am now writing up the report.'

'I believe I now have an adequate explanation of what happened.'

'We now have a decision that this advertising campaign should go ahead.'

'We now have the plans for this new project. It is only a matter of tidying them up and laying them out formally.'

'Our negotiation has succeeded and we have an agreement.'

In all such cases the work has mostly been done. There may still be some finishing touches like drawing up the plans, writing the report, signing the agreement.

In all such cases it does not mean that the **GO** stage is unnecessary. It simply means that the **GO** stage is simple and short. A short road is still a road.

Routine Channels

You have decided which film you want to see so you go to the cinema and see the film. The action required is routine. You have chosen the house you want to buy so you go through the routine of buying it. There may be points at which you have to stop and think again, for example with financing, but the mechanisms for action are in place and are well known.

If you are working in a large organization then your role might be to make a decision or to give an order. The mechanisms are in place to carry out this order.

So at the **GO** stage you might ask yourself: 'What channels, mechanisms or routines are in place to carry out the results of my thinking?'

- There may well be routine channels which are very good.
- There may be routine channels which are barely adequate.
- There may be some routine channels but you feel you could do better.
- There may be no routine channels and you have to 'design' your own action plan.

The Design of Action

In my book *Opportunities*,* I introduced the notion of *if-boxes*. Action could be divided into those things which were entirely under your control and those things which had to await some 'outcome'.

You could get into a car and drive to a shop with the intention of buying a certain brand of computer. That much is under your control. *If* the shop has the computer you would buy it. *If* the shop did not have the computer you would ask where to get it and drive to the next shop. The *design* of action means having as much as possible under your control and also designing the action that you would take after the *if-box*, whichever way the outcome of that box were to go.

So if you sat at home and phoned up various computer stores

**Opportunities*, Penguin Books, 1978.

to see which one carried the brand you wanted, you would save yourself a lot of driving time.

Of course, life is full of of small 'ifs'. In the above example you might have said:

- if the car starts
- if the car has enough fuel
- if I find a place to park
- if the shop is open.

We ignore these small 'ifs' and concentrate on the larger ones.

So we can divide action into:

- this I can do
- this depends on an outcome (if-box).

The if-box may mean asking for information. The if-box may mean asking someone to do something. The if-box may be a search which may or may not be successful.

Sometimes if-boxes are so important that they become a whole new thinking focus in their own right.

Often an if-box means investigating the feasibility, the acceptance or the cost. You could ask your employees if they would like to organize access to the car park. They may accept this idea or reject it. To build up business for your new restaurant you might employ a publicist. But you would first have to find a good publicist who was willing to work with you for the fee you were willing to pay.

Sometimes the outputs from an if-box are known in advance.

There are two possible roads. If one is not usable then I take the other. If there is no plane to get me to Paris at the right time then I could take the train through the tunnel. I might set out to look for a substance with certain characteristics. The search may reveal such a substance or may indicate that there is no such substance.

At other times the output is not known. I can put up a work of art at auction but cannot know what price I shall get. If the price is high then I can buy a house in France. If the price is low then I shall invest in the stock market. I could put a figure to separate 'high' from 'low'.

It is within your control to advertise your services as a consultant or as a gardener. The output is not under your control. You may be flooded with inquiries or you may get very few.

STAGES

Action planning usually involves stages.

In the old days pilgrims used to stop at defined points along the defined pilgrimage route. These stops were for refreshment, for rest and for sleeping. So there can be stages along a defined route. These stages are there as *targets*, as checkpoints and as summaries.

'*We have ended the first stage.*'

'*We are now at this point.*'

'*Our immediate goal is as follows . . .*'

'*We are still on track.*'

Such stages are points along a well-defined track. But there are other types of stages.

There may be a point at which several things come together and unless those things come together you cannot proceed further. These are a sort of 'if-boxes'. 'Unless you pass your law examination we cannot proceed.' At a certain point the plans and resources may have to come together. Such stages put us in a position to move forward. These stages are not just stops along a way but *assembly points*.

I can design an advertisement and pay for its insertion in a newspaper. I cannot foretell the outcome but if there is no mechanism for dealing with the replies then I am wasting my time and money. So that stage has to be prepared in advance.

OBJECTIVES AND SUB-OBJECTIVES

The overall objective, target or destination may be well known. It is difficult, however, to design actions simply to reach that overall target. For example, you are heading north and come to a blocked road. You have to design your action locally. It is no longer enough to insist that you keep heading north. On a local basis you may have to head south in order to get by the obstruction.

For such reasons and also for reasons of motivation and checking we usually set up *sub-objectives*. These are destinations on the way to the final destination. There is such a sub-objective at the end of each stage of the action design. In the overall design these sub-objectives are designed to get us to the final destination. So at any moment it is enough to head towards the sub-objective. If we reach each sub-objective in sequence we shall eventually reach the final destination.

Even as we head towards the sub-objective we need to keep the final destination in mind somewhere. The reason is that an action taken to achieve a sub-objective may make impossible the overall objective. A boy is taking some chickens to market. On the way he decides to sell some of the chickens to pay for his lodging. When he does finally get to market there are no more chickens to sell. So the whole purpose of his journey has been removed. That is an exaggeration, but if we do not keep the overall objective in mind then we might take actions that satisfy the immediate sub-objective but not the overall objective.

FLEXIBILITY AND ROUTINE

In my book *Six Action Shoes*,* I describe six basic styles of action:

- navy formal shoes: routine action
- brown brogues: enterprise action
- grey running shoes: investigative action
- orange rubber boots: crisis action
- pink slippers: human-values action
- purple riding boots: authority role action.

It is not possible to train someone to be perfect in all different situations. So the intention is to lay out very clearly certain basic styles of action. Then in any situation you use one or

**Six Action Shoes*, HarperCollins, 1992.

combine two styles of action. For example, it may be a crisis with a great need for human-values action.

At this point we are looking at the difference between routine action (navy formal shoes) and enterprise action (brown brogues). There are times when the action needs to be exactly routine. A pilot with a pre-flight check-list will need to go through the routine precisely or he may take off with insufficient fuel.

At other times there is a need for flexibility. The target or objective is set. There are certain guidelines or limits (keep within this cost, do nothing illegal) but the person is allowed to design his or her own way of getting to the objective. Depending on local circumstances and depending on personal style, different people may design different courses of action. Flexibility may be less extensive. There may be a routine laid out but if there is an obstacle or a change, then the person has permission to become flexible. The Ritz Carlton hotel chain had a policy that any employee was authorized to spend up to $2,000 to put right a mistake that had inconvenienced a hotel guest.

There is always a dilemma. The more that can be set down to routine the easier action becomes. On the other hand, the stronger the routine, the more difficult it becomes to deal with changes and local difficulties.

Always keep in mind that there is no shame and much value in using set routines. At the same time you must keep in mind the possibility of being flexible. If there are unexpected roadworks you may have to find another route.

CHECKS AND MONITORING

How do we know that we are still 'on track'? In the old days navigators would periodically take sightings from the stars to check where they were. Today they use satellite signals which tell even quite a small boat exactly where it is at any moment.

One of the reasons for designing action in stages is that we can check what is happening. Are we doing what we set out to do? Are the results at this point what we estimated them to be? Do we carry on with the same plan or do we change it?

If your efforts to attract people to the restaurant do not seem to be succeeding, do you try harder in the same direction or try something different? This is always a difficult question because results are usually not as immediate as we expect. The restaurant may gradually be getting better known but has not reached that threshold where everyone wants to be seen there.

Any action is designed into the future. Only description is in the past. So we cannot be certain about the future. There is risk. Things may not turn out as expected. There may even be unforeseen disasters.

We may need to monitor the money being spent on a research project. Research projects are almost always under-funded. This is because things always seem easier before you start doing them. Also those asking for the budget pitch it too low in order to get approval. We may need to monitor the expenditure of a building contractor, who may also underestimate the cost in order to get the contract.

At some point you may need to terminate the research project or modify the building or fire the contractor. Without a monitoring procedure you would never have known when to do this.

FALL-BACK POSITIONS

Things may not work out as anticipated. We may have been over-optimistic. Conditions may have changed. Competitors may have responded fiercely. We may simply have got it wrong.

Do we start thinking again at this point? Or, have we prepared in advance for this possibility? Have we prepared a fall-back position or a fall-back strategy. The term originates in military strategy. If the attack does not succeed what is the fall-back position? This could also apply to defence. If the first line of defence crumbles what is the fall-back position?

Even if you decide to do some new thinking at the moment you realize that things are not working out as hoped, it is still valuable to have a fall-back strategy. You are not obliged to use it. Your thinking at the moment may come up with a strategy better suited to the new circumstances. At the same time, you have the comfort of knowing that there is a strategy ready to be used if you do not come up with a better one.

There are at least three ways of dealing with risk:

1. Seek to reduce the risk (design or protection)
2. Compensation if things go wrong
3. A fall-back position.

The fall-back position suggests a *defensive* or *second-best* strategy. This need not be the case. The new strategy may also be an attacking strategy. If the market has changed in a certain way then let us profit from this new market. This means designing strategies that will work whichever way things go (no-lose strategies). I am not suggesting that this is easy because it is not. But we can set out to think in that way.

If people are not building new houses in a recession then they will be spending more money on refurbishing old houses. So let us set up a division which specializes in refurbishment. If people are not holidaying at home then they are holidaying abroad, so let us also get into that business. If people are not buying newspapers, but are content with magazines or television, then let us get into those businesses.

People

It is fairly obvious that 'people' are much more involved in the action side of thinking than in the pure thinking side. Many thinkers work in the abstract as they might in mathematics. In mathematics people do not matter. In action people do.

The OPV tool in the CoRT thinking lessons directs attention to the people involved in the situation. The Red Hat allows people to express their feelings.

Most action involves a lot of people.

ACCEPTANCE

There are those who have to accept the idea or proposal. They have their own agendas, politics and *logic bubbles*.

A 'logic bubble' is that set of perceptions, feelings and interests within which a person acts totally logically (see *Practical Thinking**).

So there are decision-makers who have to accept the idea or proposal. You have to work at a personal level with them. It is often not much use just explaining why the idea is so very good. You have to link it in to their fears and ambitions. You may even have to invite them to contribute to the idea so that they feel involved. It hardly needs saying that 'egos' are heavily involved. So are territorial or turf considerations.

One executive in Brussels told me how he had fought hard to produce a computer 'handbook' for his department. Permission was always refused because producing 'handbooks' was the work of the computer department. One day he woke up in the morning and decided he was not going to produce a handbook after all; he was going to produce a 'manual'. There was no problem with this.

The *pink slipper* action mode comes in here. People are what they are. There is no point in hoping that they could be something else. Complaining will rarely make that change a reality.

**Practical Thinking*, Penguin Books, 1977.

Good salespeople learn how to deal with people the way they are. They do not return to the office and complain that people out there are very stupid. If they are so stupid then it should be easy to sell to them!

Creative people often put the emphasis on the novelty of an idea. Novelty is of value to the creative ego, but novelty is only increased risk to anyone who has to take responsibility for using the idea. Far better to downplay the novelty and put all the emphasis on the 'benefits' of the idea. In most organizations 'me-too' ideas are also much more easily accepted than brand-new ones. A 'me-too' idea is your copying of an idea being successfully introduced by someone else.

MOTIVATION

You need people to help you carry out the idea or even to carry out the idea for you. Why should they be motivated? Why should they want the bother of doing something new when there was comfort in the old things?

It is always very difficult for a motivated person to understand the lack of motivation of others. Most people are content with complacency and maintenance. Why change? Change means disruption and risk. The outcome is not certain but the disruption is certain.

No one wants to assume that everyone is 'greedy' and only asks, 'What is in it for me?' Even if this is not widespread on the actual bribery level, it is widespread on the psychological level.

A few people are naturally motivated by new ideas and change. Without change such people are bored.

It may be possible to put across the excitement of change to other people. At the same time there is a need to reduce the disruption.

It is easy enough to say that people should get involved and 'buy into' the idea. This is harder to do in practice than in theory. When the bandwagon does pick up speed, however, people clamber aboard. They no longer want to be left behind.

So seek out those that are motivated. Build up a growing group of motivated people and then hope for the bandwagon effect.

OBSTACLES

People can be obstacles. People in positions of authority can block ideas or fail to support them. People lower down the chain can give lip-service to an idea and then allow it quietly to die. At all levels there can be active opposition or passive opposition. Passive opposition is actually worse. Active opposition can be faced and confronted. People may have to change jobs. Passive opposition is often not noticed at all – but the new idea simply does not work. It is very difficult to pinpoint why and where it is not working. It may be necessary to give someone responsibility, at all levels, for making the idea work.

INCENTIVES AND EXPECTATIONS

Some organizations reward people for creative suggestions. This has a value because incentives usually have a value. It may, however, have a counter-productive effect. People who feel that their ideas are never going to be good enough to be rewarded do not even try.

Research has shown that the best sort of incentive is not money or time, but recognition. People want to be noticed by their fellows, by management and by the organization as a whole. So highlighting behaviour is a powerful source of motivation.

Expectations are very different from incentives. In any organization people are very good at playing the 'game' the way they perceive the 'rules' to be written. The smart students at school learn how to please the teacher, how to pass tests and how to copy when required. They succeed because they are good at assessing the game and then at playing the game. The best people in organizations behave in the same way. They learn the 'game'. What behaviour is rewarded? What behaviour is punished? What behaviour is ignored?

Within an organization this 'game' is called 'culture'. Sometimes this culture is set by leadership. A dynamic leader can really change a culture. Sometimes the culture has built up over a number of years. A new leader may try to change the culture but nothing really happens apart from a few cosmetic changes.

For 'game' read 'culture'. For 'culture' read 'expectations'. Expectations are very powerful indeed. People are driven by expectations. Expectations determine how you fit into the world around. In Japan most behaviour is determined by the expectations of the group around.

Expectations are more powerful than incentives. If there is an expectation that people should be creative, then they will seek to be creative at every possible opportunity. Everyone will try and meet this expectation. That is why the green hat is so powerful as part of the Six Hats framework. When the green hat is in use then everyone at the meeting is expected to be creative. If you sit there saying nothing while everyone around you is trying to be creative, then you are seen to be deficient. This is quite different from 'rewarding' creativity. Reward makes creativity seem something 'extra' and you do not have to do it. Expectation means that it is not extra at all and you are expected to do it.

EFFECTIVENESS

Some people are effective and some people are not. Effectiveness is a very rare quality. It is a quality that is not sufficiently noticed or attended to. Yet in the end effectiveness is the most important quality for action.

Effective people get on with things and do them. Less effective people have to keep coming back for encouragement and instruction. Less effective people seek out reasons for not doing something. Effective people hardly notice the obstacles. They just step around them.

In my experience, I have come across really effective people at low levels and also really ineffective people at quite high levels. It is not a matter of intelligence. It may not even be a matter of personality. It seems to be a set of internal expectations. If you set out to do something, then you do it.

If other people are involved in helping you carry out the

actions of the **GO** stage then you might want to select effective people.

TASK FORCES AND GROUPS

It is lonely to work on your own, especially if you are trying to do something outside the normal routine. Most people prefer to work in groups. There are then people with whom to discuss things. There is mutual support when things get difficult. There is the exchange of ideas. Loners are more easily ignored by groups. People can be asked to join a group to ensure their support for the change.

Another advantage of the task force is that it is set up specifically to reach some objective. There is a focus upon that objective. Task-force members may have other duties and other functions but the 'task force' as an animal in its own right has one purpose. There is therefore much more sense of making or failing to make progress towards the objective than there might be with individuals.

'*How far have we got?*'

'*Have we achieved anything?*'

'*What are the plans?*'

'*What do we do next?*'

Against these great advantages of the special group there are some negative points. If a function is tied up in a 'special' group then others tend to feel that it is no longer their business. Let the special group get on with it. The group becomes isolated and detached.

For example, setting up a special 'creative' group may indicate to others that they do not need to be creative or that they are not capable of being creative or that the creative 'function' is now being taken care of.

For these reasons any special group must keep in close interaction with everyone else.

In politics, a well-known strategy for 'doing something' when you intend to do nothing is to set up a 'special committee'. The matter is then being taken care of. That answer can be given to any question. Something is indeed 'happening'. So everyone forgets all about it. Eventually the report of the special committee is published without any fanfare and nothing changes. Task forces can sometimes be seen in the same light.

EXPERTS

There is no need to make jokes about amateur brain surgeons in order to emphasize the importance of experts.

In terms of knowledge, the expert is someone who has made it his business or her business to collect and to digest information in a particular field. So there is both the information of personal experience and the information gained from others. An expert can also direct your search by suggesting where you look. It would be very difficult to pick up all this expertise, although computer networks do now allow someone infinitely more access to information than ever before.

So you go to any expert to seek information and to find out where to get information.

Experts have also learned how to ask the important questions. You ask questions when you are ignorant, but if you are truly ignorant you cannot ask the right questions.

In terms of action an expert is someone who has refined the action so that all unnecessary bits have been thrown out. A novice does something in a cumbersome way. The expert does it more simply. The novice goes from A to B to get to C. The expert goes from A directly to C.

What about judgement?

This is a much more difficult matter. The expert's judgement is based on the past. The expert's judgement is based on *what is* rather than on *what can be*. The expert is always being asked for competent expert opinions. The expert cannot risk his or her reputation. So the expert does need to stay on the side of caution. Better to say that something cannot be done than to say that it can be done and to be responsible for some mistake. Experts are the guardians of the past and people expect them to be so.

Of course, experts do vary. There are those experts who keep the curiosity of an open mind. They are willing to open up 'possibilities' instead of preferring to trade in certainties. These are experts who have added wisdom to their expertise.

Expert systems transferred to a computer provide the computer with the complex judgement system that an expert will have built up over many years. The computer becomes as good as the expert. This is different from neural-net expertise where the computer network builds up its own expertise through its own experience (helped by training).

Experts once said that to get a rocket to the moon it would have to weigh one million tons. Experts once calculated that the total world market for computers would be just eight computers. Experts once declared that the telephone was nothing more than an electronic toy. It is possible to go on with such stories.

What such stories illustrate is that experts are experts in what has been but not in what may be. Much of the time our behaviour does need to be guided by what has been. Only a very small part of our behaviour needs to consider the creative possibilities of what might be. A journey may consist of hundreds of miles. Changing a road may only involve a few yards. That change may be vital. So creative change is vital. But we should never forget that the hundreds of miles depends on past experience.

So, as with all things that are mainly good but occasionally restricting, it becomes a matter of balance. Use the thing for its good points, but also be aware of the dangers. Fire can burn down buildings but we use fire for cooking. Knives can cut throats but we use knives to cut the bread. Too much salt makes food taste terrible but we use salt on food. So experts are wonderfully useful, but do not get put off a new idea by an expert judgement. But also remember that the expert might be right. No one has yet invented a perpetual motion machine.

Energy

Action requires energy. The design of action might be fine. The motivation might be in order. But where is the energy to come from?

Energy, like effectiveness, is one of those intangible things which is impossible to test or measure, so we forget all about it because the scientific system has decided that what is not measurable does not matter.

You get on a train and sit back and read. The train is providing the energy to get to your chosen destination.

You drive a car to the destination. You now have to put in the energy of 'driving' and control.

You ride a bicycle. You now have to put in the energy of finding the way, controlling the bicycle and working the pedals.

You walk to your destination. You provide all the energy without any of the amplification provided by the bicycle.

With action you can plug into a system that will provide all the energy you require. If you buy space for a newspaper advertisement then the 'newspaper mechanism' will provide all the energy of distribution. This is a good deal easier than word of mouth or seeking to tell everyone personally.

With the design of action we seek to plug into systems that can provide the energy of action. When you cannot achieve something directly you may want to plug into the energy of the lawcourts to make something happen. You may hire people to do things for you.

AMPLIFICATION

You only have so much energy yourself. How can you amplify that energy?

Many successful entrepreneurs who were interviewed for my book *Tactics** had partners who helped them. Often the partner looked after the financial and administrative side while the entrepreneur had the ideas and vision. Partnership is a very common way of mutiplying energy.

On a higher level, strategic alliances are another way of multiplying energy. Why not join forces with another organization that has a lot of energy in the field?

Cooperation is another multiplier of energy. When the Japanese food suppliers decided to cooperate on the distribution of food to food stores they reduced the distribution costs by 80 per cent. Instead of each supplier's van going to each store with a quarter of a load, one van went with a full load. Danish magazine publishers cooperate to own a distribution system that distributes all their competing magazines.

Western corporations seek to get suppliers to reduce costs by using competition. You tell all your suppliers that you will only buy from the supplier with the lowest costs. So suppliers compete to lower their costs. Japanese corporations do it

* *Tactics: The Art and Science of Success*, HarperCollins, 1981.

differently. They go to their long-term suppliers with whom they have built up a long-term relationship. They discuss the need to lower costs. Then they send their own people to help the supplier reduce costs.

Competition and cooperation are not the opposites which many people believe them to be. You are running an antiques shop. Someone opens another antiques shop just next to yours. Some of your customers seem to be diverted to this new shop. That is competition. What should you do? Probably you should invite a third party to open yet another antiques shop. Why? Because it then becomes an 'antiques market'. Buyers know that there are several antiques shops in that area. So more buyers come to the area and all the shops do better. They are still competing against each other.

Negotiations are usually seen as adversarial. The parties are fighting each other. Yet there are points where the interests of both are aligned. If productivity can be increased, the selling price can be lowered and the market will grow. That will ensure the future of the company and the possibility of improving wages.

Theoretically, both sides in a lawcourt are seeking the truth – that is the purpose of the argument system. In fact it ends up as 'case-making'. Each side wants to win. If one side finds out something which would help the case of the other side, then that something will not be revealed. This would not occur in those countries which have an 'investigative' rather than an 'adversarial' legal system.

So designing the 'energy' into the action plan is an important part of the **GO** stage of thinking. Where is the energy to come from? Energy is not just resources but the use of those resources.

Planning

It has been mentioned several times that the desired output of the whole thinking process might be a plan. A town planner seeks to end up with a plan. A chef seeks to end up with a meal plan. A tour operator seeks to end up with a tour plan. A fund-raising committee seeks to end up with a detailed plan. In all such cases the 'plan' is the desired end result.

At other times the plan is the final part of the thinking. How do we put this problem solution to work? How do we take this creative idea further? How do we carry out this design? Here the plan is part of the **GO** stage of thinking.

Action usually seems simple. We do one thing after another. At each point we shall know what to do next.

Experience has taught me, in so many ways, that spelling out and doing deliberately what seems obvious and easy makes a huge difference. Earlier in the book I mentioned how people who prided themselves on their comprehensive judgement produced a far fuller result when using the Yellow and Black Hats deliberately and formally. Many highly creative people have told me how they get the best ideas when using the techniques of lateral thinking in a deliberate, step-by-step way.

So there is value in laying out the action plan. That is why investors always want entrepreneurs to lay out their business plans. When you have something down in front of you it is very different from that something existing in your head. You are forced to confront the gaps. You are forced to make decisions. You are forced to make estimates and guesses.

One way of getting young children (five to twelve) to develop their constructive thinking is to ask them to make drawings. How would you weigh an elephant? How would you exercise a dog? How would you build a house more quickly? Drawings force the child to confront a need and to offer a solution (see my book *Children Solve Problems**).

So lay out the plan in terms of steps and stages. Indicate which are the routine channels that can be used and which are the uncertainties or 'if-boxes'. Indicate the sub-objectives. What is being aimed for at every moment? Indicate the checkpoints or the results that would need to be considered at those checkpoints. Put in alternative strategies and fall-back positions.

People are frightened of making plans because they feel they would then be restricted by that plan. This need not be so. The plan itself is never restrictive. The way you use the plan may be restrictive. Again we are back to one of those situations where there are mainly good points but some dangers. Be aware of the dangers but use the good points. So make a plan. Change it when you wish. Deviate from it when there is good reason. Scrap the original plan and make a better one if this seems the right thing to do.

**Children Solve Problems*, Penguin Books, 1972.

Summary of the GO Stage of Thinking

Thinking and action are not separate. Thinking should continue into the action stage. The output of thinking must be put into the real world. It is not enough to think of a solution to a problem. You also need to consider how that solution will be put into action.

The purpose of the **GO** stage of thinking is to take the output from the **SO** stage and to think about putting this to work. The **GO** stage is all about making things happen.

We look at mechanisms and routines for action. We look at uncertainties and 'if-boxes'. We look at the many people factors. We look at the role of experts. We consider the 'energy' of action. We suggest the usefulness of an action plan even if it is to be altered later.

It is true that sometimes the **GO** stage is simple and short because the desired outcome of the thinking is information, understanding or a decision.

I want to reverse the usual emphasis, which says that most thinking does not require action, to saying that most thinking should include action – but there may be exceptions.

Situation Coding

There can be a value, sometimes, in having a simple way of describing a *thinking situation* or *thinking need* to yourself or to others.

'*It is this type of situation.*'

'*This is the sort of thinking that is required.*'

'*How would you describe the situation?*'

'*What thinking do we need here?*'

In this section I intend to describe a simple type of situation coding. This is a subjective coding and is not a formal classification of situations.

You use this coding to indicate how the situation seems to you. Someone else might disagree and then you can both focus on the disagreement.

Even though you may start out coding a situation one way, you may find that you need to modify the code as you go along.

The Coding

For each of the five stages of thinking (**TO**, **LO**, **PO**, **SO**, **GO**) you apply a number from 1 to 9.

This 'rating' from 1 to 9 indicates the *amount*, the *difficulty* or the *importance* of the thinking that needs to be done in that stage.

For example, if you are asked to choose between a fixed set of alternatives then the **PO** stage does not require much thinking because the alternatives have been given. So the **PO** stage gets a 1. On the other hand, the **SO** stage is going to have to do a lot of work so this stage gets a 9. The **GO** stage may also have quite a lot to do and gets a 6. The **TO** stage does not require much work because the thinking purpose has been clearly set, so the **TO** stage gets a 1. The **LO** stage is important because you need to explore perceptions and find information in order to make your choice. So the **LO** stage gets an 8.

The overall coding now becomes 18/196. The break after the first two digits is for ease of pronunciation: one eight / one nine six.

In another situation there seems to be confusion. The information is present but you do not know what to do. Perhaps the emotional factor is high. The emphasis may now fall on the **TO** stage.

'Am I clear as to what I want to achieve? What is the real purpose of my thinking? With what do I want to end up?'

So the **TO** stage gets a 9. The information is mostly available, so the **LO** stage gets a 4. The **PO** stage does require some work but if the **TO** stage is clear then the **PO** stage will not be difficult. So the **PO** stage also gets a 4. The **SO** stage may be important, especially if there is emotional involvement, so this stage gets a 6. The **GO** stage may be straightforward and gets a 1.

So the final coding becomes: 94/461 (nine four / four six one).

On another occasion the sole purpose of the thinking is to obtain a specific piece of information. The **TO** stage is clear, so this gets a 1. The **LO** stage is all important and gets a 9. The **PO** stage is also important because we may have to consider possible ways of getting the information. So the **PO** stage gets an 8. The **SO** stage may be simple if there turns out to be one clear way of getting the information. But this may not be clear and there may be several ways to choose between. So the **SO** stage gets a 5. The **GO** stage is relatively simple and gets a 4.

The overall coding becomes: 19/854 (one nine / eight five four).

Another situation is a direct creative demand. You are asked to come up with a good name for a book. The purpose of the thinking is very clear, so the **TO** stage gets a 1. The information stage is important because you need to know what is in the book, who it is meant to appeal to and where it will be sold. You also need to know the titles of other books on the same subject. So the **LO** stage is important and gets an 8. Obviously, most of the work is going to be creatively in the **PO** stage, so this gets a 9. The choice stage is going to be difficult. How do we decide which title to use? So the **SO** stage also gets an 8. The **GO** stage is simple because if you have selected the title you simply use that title. So the **GO** stage gets a 1.

The resulting coding is: 18/981 (one eight / nine eight one).

Only use the 9 rating once in the coding even if two stages both seem very important. The 9 should indicate the *most important* stage. The other figures should be used as often as you like.

Of course, all stages of thinking are important and you may be inclined to give a high rating to each of the five stages. This would be to misunderstand the purpose of the coding. A stage with a low rating does not mean that stage is unimportant. It means that that stage will require less thinking work than other stages. It is relative. If you are set a specific task then the **TO** stage is simple. If you simply wish to make a choice then the **GO** stage may be simple. If you are working in a closed problem where all the information is available then the **LO** stage may be simple. If you are presented with fixed alternatives then the **PO** stage may be simple. If you clearly identify a situation in the **PO** stage then the **SO** stage may be simple.

In a negotiation situation the purpose may be clear: 'We want to end up with an agreement acceptable by both sides.' So the **TO** stage is simple and gets a 1.

The information stage may have to explore a lot of information. There will also be a need to explore values, fears, perceptions, etc. So this stage will be important and the **LO** stage gets an 8.

The **PO** stage is key because it is here that the 'design' of possible outcomes has to be worked out. There will need to be a lot of activity here. So the **PO** stage gets the 9.

It is difficult to predict how much work will need to be done in the **SO** stage. If one of the possible designs put forward in the **PO** stage is very good then there will not be much difficulty choosing this outcome. But if there is no one outstanding design then the choice process is going to be hard work. So the **SO** stage gets an 8.

The desired outcome of the thinking is an acceptable agreement. But some thinking should also be given to its implementation. So the **GO** stage gets a 5.

The final coding becomes: 18/985 (one eight / nine eight five).

If there is a problem to be solved then you may need to spend time defining and redefining the problem. So the **TO** stage should not be automatic and deserves a 6. This is particularly so if the problem has been around for a long time.

If the problem has been around for a long time the information may be well known, so the **LO** stage may also get a 6.

The generative effort has to take place in the **PO** stage so this gets the 9.

The **SO** stage may be simple if a solution has turned up in the **PO** stage. If no solution has turned up then the **SO** stage is also simple because all possibilities will be rejected. So the **SO** stage gets a 5.

The implementation of the solution needs thinking through, so the **GO** stage gets a 7.

The final coding becomes: 66/957 (six six / nine five seven).

Should Be

The coding is not just a simple description of what is the case but an indication of what you believe the situation 'should be'.

When you are given a problem to solve, the definition of the problem may also be given to you. This could mean that the **TO** stage only merits a 1. But if you feel that much more attention should be given to defining, redefining and even breaking down the problem then you should indicate a 7 or an 8 – in some cases even the 9.

In this way the suggested coding becomes not only an indication of the situation but also a 'strategy' for dealing with the situation.

If you really feel that a thorough information search is going to solve the problem then you would want to give the 9 to the **LO** stage.

If you really feel that only creative effort will solve the problem then you give the 9 to the **PO** stage.

If you feel that there are already enough possibilities and choice is required then you give the 9 to the **SO** stage.

If you feel that the action design will be most important (an acceptance difficulty) then the **GO** stage gets the 9.

A 91/811 situation means that the thinker believes that a clear definition of the thinking purpose is all important. The information is simple and available. There is a need to generate possibilities. The thinker believes that a satisfactory possibility will be forthcoming so the **SO** and **GO** stages will be simple.

An 18/195 situation seems to be a decision situation: perhaps a go/no go situation. The purpose is clear. Information is important. There is little need to generate possibilities. The **SO** stage is all-important and the action stage is moderately important.

Summary

In this section I have suggested a simple form of descriptive coding for thinking situations. This coding consists of assigning a 1 to 9 rating to each of the five stages of thinking. The higher the rating the more 'thinking work' there is to be done in this stage.

The coding indicates what you think should be the case. The coding indicates your intended thinking strategy.

You can use the coding to describe a thinking need to yourself or to describe it to others.

The coding becomes a way of thinking about and talking about a whole situation.

Summary

At the beginning of the book I wrote that it was my intention to put forward a simple and effective method for thinking. At different times it may have seemed to the reader that matters were getting rather more complicated. They need not be.

Think only of the basic framework. That is what you need to use. You can read and reread each section to learn more about each stage. Treat the sections as *reference* sections which you can go back to.

It is best to use the framework in a very simple way at first and then gradually to elaborate each stage. This is much better than trying to use each stage in its full sense from the beginning.

There are times when some of the thinking refers to business situations rather than to personal thinking. Those who are only interested in personal thinking should ignore these items. But many readers of the book will need to do some of their thinking in the business world, so that aspect does need attending to in the book.

The strategy for the reader is to be selective. Pick out those things which you can understand and which you feel you can handle. Be aware of the other material but do not feel you need to use everything at once.

It is not a matter of reading the book and then putting it down and never looking at it again. You will need reminding. You will not get the most out of your thinking unless you eventually do attend to the matters in the book. A superficial knowledge is enough to get started, but not enough to build up an effective thinking skill.

As usual, some readers and most critics will assume that, because the bare bones of the framework are simple, the whole approach is too simple and is indeed something they have always done. In my experience this arrogantly complacent attitude to thinking is always misplaced. Many people who consider themselves to be good thinkers are using only one approach: analysis, judgement and identification. This is only one part of thinking and leaves out the whole creative, generative and productive side of thinking.

The Five Stages of Thinking

The five stages will be summarized below. The key points will be given.

TO

'Where am I going to?'

What is the purpose of my thinking? With what do I want to end up? This stage of thinking is very important indeed. We usually give this stage too little attention. We need to be very clear on what we are thinking about and what we want to achieve. We need to define and redefine the purpose. We need to seek alternative definitions. We may want to break down the purpose into smaller ones.

There are two main types of purpose or focus. In the traditional *purpose* focus we set out what we want to achieve. This may be solving a problem, achieving an objective, carrying out a task or making an improvement in a defined direction. In the *area* focus, we simply define the area in which we are looking for new ideas.

Keep very clearly in mind that solving problems and putting right defects is only one aspect of thinking. There is far more to thinking than problem solving.

LO

'Lo and behold.'

What can we see? What should we look for? In this stage we seek to gather and to lay out the information we need for our thinking. The search for information should be very broad at times but at other times it may need to be focused. There are *fishing questions*, where we do not know what answer will emerge. There are *shooting questions*, where the answer is a 'yes' or a 'no' and we are checking things out.

Sometimes we need a guess or a hypothesis in order to know where to look. Use such guesses but be careful not to be trapped by them.

Perceptions and values are an important part of this stage. What are the different perceptions? How can things be looked at differently? What values are involved? Do different people have different values? What is the thinking of different people?

PO

'Let's generate some possibilities.'

This is the creative, productive and generative stage of thinking. It is in this stage that we put forward 'possibilities'. It is this stage which links up the purpose of our thinking with the output of our thinking. There are two thinking stages before and two afterwards. This stage is the link between input and output.

There are four broad approaches that can be used in the **PO** stage.

1. *Search for routine.* Here we seek to identify the situation so that we can then know what to do and can apply the action that has been established as the routine response to that situation. This is the traditional approach to thinking.

2. *General approach.* Here we link starting-point and desired result with a broad, 'general' concept. Then we seek to narrow this down to give us specific ideas that we can use. The Concept Fan is part of this approach. We work backwards, in general terms, from where we want to be in order to produce ideas that we can use.

3. *Creative approach.* Here we set out deliberately to generate ideas and then we seek to modify these ideas to fit our needs. There are the formal techniques of lateral thinking such as provocation and the use of a random entry. 'Movement' is a key part of creative thinking. We 'move' forward from a provocation to get a useful idea.

4. *Design and assembly.* Here we lay out the needs and ingredients in parallel. Then we seek to design a way forward to

achieve the 'design brief'. We seek to assemble or to put things together to give us what we want.

The purpose of the **PO** stage is to be generative and to produce multiple possibilities.

SO
'So what is the outcome?'

The purpose of the **SO** stage is to take the multiple possibilities produced by the **PO** stage and to reduce these to a usable outcome.

There is the *development* stage, in which we seek to build up and improve ideas. We seek to remove defects.

Then there is the *evaluation and assessment* stage, in which we examine each idea. We seek to list the benefits and values. We seek to list the difficulties and problems.

Next is the *choice* stage. We now lay out all the competing ideas and choose between them. There are various methods for making this choice. We may use one method to narrow down the number of alternatives and then use direct comparison.

The *decision* process is concerned with whether or not we do something. We need to consider the decision frame and the pressures. We must consider the need for the decision. We must consider the risks.

At the end of the **SO** stage we may have an idea we want to use or we may have nothing.

GO

'Go to it!'

The **GO** stage is concerned with action. How is the chosen idea going to be put into action? What is the action design?

There are stages and sub-objectives. There is the need to monitor and to check.

We use routine channels and we assess the uncertainties with *if-boxes*.

The *people factor* in its various forms is a key part of action. People need persuading. Ideas must be accepted. There is a need for motivation. People can be obstructive. All these things need to be considered.

There is also the need to design in the *energy of action*. Where is this to come from?

Simpler

An even simpler summary would go as follows:

TO: What do I want to do?

LO: What information do I have (and need)?

PO: How do I get there?

SO: Which alternative do I choose?

GO: How do I put this into action?

Backwards and Forwards

The five stages of thinking are not sealed compartments. When you have moved on from one stage to the next you can still go back to an earlier stage.

For example, when working in the **PO** stage you may find you need some specific information. So you return to the **LO** stage. Or you may find that you want to redefine the situation. So you return to the **TO** stage.

Do not overdo this moving backwards and forwards or you will lose all the advantages of having set stages and you will return to the confusion of ordinary thinking where one idea follows another without any discipline or structure.

Enjoy Your Thinking Skill

Thinking does not only have to be about complicated problems and puzzles. Thinking is not only valid when matters are very difficult.

Enjoy thinking about simple things where you will get answers. In that way you will build up your skill in thinking, your confidence in that skill and your enjoyment of that skill.

Because something is easy does not mean that it is not worth doing. It is better to do something easy and to do it really well than to seek only to do difficult things and not to succeed at all.

Far too many people are put off the enjoyment of thinking because they have been led to believe that thinking should be difficult. It does not have to be.

EDWARD DE BONO

LATERAL THINKING

The classic work about improving creativity

In schools we are taught to meet problems head-on: what Edward de Bono calls 'vertical thinking'. This works well in simple situations – but we are at a loss when this approach fails. What then?

Lateral thinking is all about freeing up your imagination. Through a series of special techniques, in groups or working alone, Edward de Bono shows how to stimulate the mind in new and exciting ways.

Soon you will be looking at problems from a variety of angles and offering up solutions that are as ingenious as they are effective. You will become much more productive and a formidable thinker in your own right.

'If more bankers and traders had read Lateral Thinking and applied the ideas of Edward de Bono to their own narrow definitions of risk, reward and human expectations, I suspect we would be in much better shape than we are'
Sir Richard Branson

EDWARD DE BONO

SIX THINKING HATS

The classic work about meetings and decision-making

Meetings are a crucial part of all our lives, but too often they go nowhere and waste valuable time. In Six Thinking Hats, Edward de Bono shows how meetings can be transformed to produce quick, decisive results every time.

The Six Hats method is a devastatingly simple technique based on the brain's different modes of thinking. The intelligence, experience and information of everyone is harnessed to reach the right conclusions quickly.

These principles have been adopted by businesses and governments around the world, ending conflict and confusion in favour of harmony and productivity.

The Six Hats strategy will fundamentally change the way you work and interact.

'An inspiring man with brilliant ideas. De Bono never ceases to amaze with his clarity of thought' Richard Branson